D0049354

WHAT MIGHT HAVE BEEN

WHAT MIGHT HAVE BEEN

**Leading Historians on Twelve
'What Ifs' of History**

Edited with an Introduction
by Andrew Roberts

Weidenfeld & Nicolson
LONDON

First published in Great Britain in 2004
by Weidenfeld & Nicolson

Introduction and compilation © 2004 Andrew Roberts
In each essay © 2004 by the writer

A CIP catalogue record for this book
is available from the British Library.

ISBN 0 297 848771

Typeset by Selwood Systems, Midsomer Norton
Printed and bound by Clays Ltd, St Ives plc

Weidenfeld & Nicolson

The Orion Publishing Group Ltd
Orion House
5 Upper Saint Martin's Lane
London WC2H 9EA

What might you be?

Contents

Contents

Acknowledgements

In the greatest of all counterfactual essay collections, *If It Had Happened Otherwise* (1931), the editor J. C. Squire wrote, 'There is nothing more tedious than the preface that panegyrises the work introduced. Every right-minded reader is indignant with attempts to dragoon him', and I agree. I would, however, like to take this opportunity to salute the splendid professionalism of my friend Amanda Foreman, who filed her pristine copy on Sunday 7 September, and then gave birth to her son Theodore the following day.

Others I would like to thank include the splendid Ion Trewin of Weidenfeld & Nicolson, my fabulous agent Georgina Capel, Sam Witherow for his fine research work, Victoria Webb for her indispensable editorial assistance, and Linden Lawson for her meticulous copy-editing. This book is dedicated to my darling daughter Cassia.

Andrew Roberts
October 2003
www.andrew-roberts.net

Notes on Contributors

Dr John Adamson is a Fellow of Peterhouse, University of Cambridge. He was educated at Trinity College, University of Melbourne, and at Christ's College, Cambridge, and studied Classics and History. His doctoral dissertation won the University of Cambridge's Seeley and Thirlwall Medals for History, and his research on the English Civil War has been awarded the Royal Historical Society's Alexander Prize. A former Visiting Fellow at Yale University and the University of California, Los Angeles, his publications include the edited volume *The Princely Courts of Europe, 1500–1750*, which was named a Book of the Year by *The Sunday Times*. His new study of the aristocracy in the English Civil War, *The Noble Revolt*, will be published in 2004.

Conrad Black is a graduate of Carleton, Laval and McGill Universities in Canada and the author of a life of Quebec's longest-serving premier, Maurice Duplessis, republished as *Render Unto Caesar*, and of the autobiographical *A Life in Progress*. His comprehensive *Franklin Delano Roosevelt: Champion of Freedom* was published in 2003. Black is the chairman of the Telegraph Group, which publishes *The Daily* and *Sunday Telegraph* and the *Spectator*, and is chairman of Hollinger International Inc., which also owns many other newspapers, including the *Chicago Sun-Times* and the *Jerusalem Post*. In a varied business career, Black has been an executive or director of many companies in many fields. He moved from Canada to Britain in 1989, and in 2001 became a life peer, as Lord Black of Crossharbour. He is also a member of the Privy Council of Canada and a Knight of the Holy See. Conrad Black is married to the author and journalist Barbara Amiel,

Black, and has three children by his former marriage. He lives in London, New York and Toronto.

Robert Cowley is the founding editor of the award-winning *MHQ: The Quarterly Journal of Military History*; he was its editor-in-chief for a decade. He has been a magazine and book editor for more than forty years and has edited a number of books that have appeared on both sides of the Atlantic: *Experience of War*, *The Osprey Companion to Military History*, *What If?*, *More What If?*, *What Ifs? of American History*, *No End Save Victory*, *With My Face to the Enemy*, and most recently *The Great War*. An authority on World War I, Cowley is writing a book on the Western Front; he has travelled its entire length from the North Sea to the Swiss border and has led tours to it. He is a graduate of Harvard, the father of four daughters, and now works out of what was a painter's studio in Connecticut, the former colony where Benedict Arnold grew up.

Amanda Foreman received her doctorate from Oxford University. She has taught at Lady Margaret Hall, Oxford; and at New York University. She is the author of *Georgiana, Duchess of Devonshire*, which won the Whitbread Prize for Best Biography in 1999. Amanda Foreman's radio and television documentaries include *Queen Victoria and the History of Sound*, *The History of the British Temperance Movement* and *Wellington's Women*. Her latest book is called *Our American Cousins: The British Volunteers in the American Civil War*. She has two children, and divides her time between London and New York.

Antonia Fraser's *The Gunpowder Plot: Terror and Faith in 1605* was published under the title *Faith and Treason: The Story of the Gunpowder Plot* in the US. It received the Crimewriters' Association Non-Fiction Gold Dagger for 1996. Her most recent biography is the internationally best-selling *Marie Antoinette: The Journey*; she has also written *Mary Queen of Scots*, *Cromwell, Our Chief of Men* and *Charles II*, as well as a short study, *King James VI and I*, in the Weidenfeld & Nicolson Kings and Queens of England series, which she edits. She has written three studies of women in history, *The Weaker Vessel*, *Boadicea's Chariot: The Warrior Queens* and *The Six Wives of Henry VIII*. Among other awards Antonia Fraser has received the James Tait Black Prize for Biography (1969), the Wolfson Award for History (1984), the Norton Medlicott Medal 2000 of the Historical Association and the Franco-British Literary Prize (2002).

David Frum's first book, *Dead Rich*, was hailed by Frank Rich in the *New York Times* as 'the smartest book ever written from the inside about the American conservative movement'. His history of the 1970s, *How We Got Here*, was praised. A former speechwriter and special assistant to President George W. Bush, Frum is the author of *The Right Man: The Surprise Presidency of George W. Bush* (2003). Now a resident fellow at the American Enterprise Institute in Washington, DC, his most recent book is *An End to Evil: How to Win the War on Terror* (2004), co-authored with Richard Perle.

Simon Heffer's books include *Like the Roman: The Life of Enoch Powell, Moral Desperado: a Life of Thomas Carlyle* and *Power and Place: The Political Consequences of King Edward VII*. He has been deputy editor and political correspondent of the *Spectator* and deputy editor of *The Daily Telegraph*. He is now a columnist and political commentator for the *Daily Mail*, and a regular contributor to the *Spectator*, the *Literary Review* and *Country Life*. Born in 1960, he read English at Cambridge University and is married with two children.

Simon Sebag Montefiore, who was born in 1965, was educated at Harrow School and then read History at Gonville and Caius College, Cambridge. He spent much of the 1990s travelling through the ex-Soviet empire, particularly in the Caucasus, Ukraine and Central Asia, and wrote widely on

Russia especially for *The Sunday Times*, *New York Times*, *New Republic* and *Spectator*. *Prince of Princes: The Life of Potemkin* was shortlisted for the Samuel Johnson, Duff Cooper and Marsh biography prizes. His latest work, *Stalin: the Court of the Red Tsar*, was published in 2003. The author of two novels and presenter of television documentaries, he lives in London with his wife, the novelist Santa Montefiore, and his daughter Lily and son Sasha.

Andrew Roberts, forty, took a First in Modern History at Gonville and Caius College, Cambridge. His biography of Neville Chamberlain's and Winston Churchill's Foreign Secretary, the Earl of Halifax, entitled *The Holy Fox*, was followed by the controversial *Eminent Churchillians*. *Salisbury: Victorian Titan*, the authorised biography of the Victorian prime minister the 3rd Marquess of Salisbury, won the Wolfson History Prize and the James Stern Silver Pen Award for Non-Fiction. He is the author of *Napoleon and Wellington*, and *Hitler and Churchill: Secrets of Leadership*, which was published in 2003. In 2001 he became a Fellow of the Royal Society of Literature. He has two children, lives in Knightsbridge and goes out with the biographer Leonie Frieda. His website can be found at www.andrew-roberts.net.

Anne Somerset was born in 1955 and read history at King's College London. Her first book, *The Life and Times of William IV*, was published in the Weidenfeld & Nicolson Kings and Queens of England series. Her second book, *Ladies-in-Waiting: From the Tudors to the Present Day*, was followed by an acclaimed biography of Elizabeth I. Her next book was a study of the poisoning of Sir Thomas Overbury in the reign of James I, entitled *Unnatural Murder*. Her most recent work, *The Affair of the Poisons*, came out in 2003. Like its predecessor it is the story of a criminal investigation and court scandal, this time set in the France of Louis XIV. Anne Somerset is married to the artist Matthew Carr and lives in London with her husband and daughter.

Norman Stone was born in Glasgow in 1941, educated at Gonville and Caius College, Cambridge and worked in Vienna and Budapest between 1963 and 1965, where he studied pre-Great-War Austria–Hungary. He taught Russian and Central European history at Cambridge, latterly as a Fellow of Trinity College, until 1984 when appointed Professor of Modern History at Oxford, in succession to Richard Cobb. In 1997 he became Professor of International Relations at Bilkent University, Ankara, and Director of the Russian–Turkish Centre. Between 1986 and 1997 he had considerable media exposure, particularly in *The Sunday Times*, but latterly also in the *Frankfurter Allgemeine Zeitung*, *Wall Street Journal* and *Cornucopia* (particularly on Turkey). His *The Eastern Front 1914–17* won the Wolfson Prize. Other publications include *Hitler*, *Europe Transformed 1878–1919* (Fontana History of Europe) and *The Other Russia*. He is currently working on *The Triumph of the Atlantic 1945–90*.

Adam Zamoyski was born in New York, but educated in Britain, at Downside and The Queen's College, Oxford. He now lives in London. A freelance historian, he has written for all the major British newspapers and periodicals as well as publishing a number of books. He is the author of two works of military history; of the best-selling history of Poland *The Polish Way*; of three biographies, which have been widely acclaimed by academics and general readers; and of the wide-ranging study of Romantic nationalism, *Holy Madness: Romantics, Patriots and Revolutionaries, 1776–1871*. His most recent book is *1812: Napoleon's Fatal March on Moscow*.

Introduction

Andrew Roberts

'Untune one string,' says Ulysses in *Troilus and Cressida*, 'And, hark! what discord follows; each thing meets in mere oppugnancy.' I believe that 'counterfactual', 'virtual' – or, more colloquially, What If? – history is starting to become much more popular; but is it merely a diverting amusement, 'fairy stories' as Simon Schama calls them, or can speculation into what did not happen historically help us in some way in the study of what actually did?

We only have to look at our own lives to appreciate how the alteration of one small thing on one particular day can sometimes have a huge effect on everything else, perhaps for years, perhaps for life. And if it is true for individuals, why should it not also hold true for history, which is but the story of the lives of millions of individuals? If you hadn't gone to that ridiculous drinks party you only attended at the last minute, for example, you might not have met the person you eventually married. If you hadn't bought that newspaper that day, you might not be doing the job you do. As an extreme example, my friend the journalist Anne Applebaum was booked on to the Lockerbie flight, but had to change her travel plans at the very last moment.

What Ifs can also ruin lives if they are allowed to. There is a television interview that Ed Murrow conducted of the Duke and Duchess of Windsor in 1956, when the veteran American broadcaster asked the exiled couple if they ever talked about 'what might have been'. They hum and hah and exchange nervous looks, before the Duke leans forward on the sofa and states categorically that they didn't. Then the Duchess, disingenuousness evident from every inflection,

1

adds: 'Don't you remember that we agreed on our honey-moon that we would make a pact never to talk about what might have been?' And the Duke quickly answers: 'Yes, we did, and we never have.' Their body language, agonised glances, tone of voice, and clunkingly clumsy lies make it perfectly clear that in fact they were tortured by their own personal What If; admittedly, under the circumstances it would have taken a superhuman effort for them not to have been.

The Gwyneth Paltrow movie *Sliding Doors* perfectly enunciates the superiority of accident versus design in history. In the film it is the closing doors of a tube train that prevent the heroine from catching her boyfriend in bed with someone else. Then a completely different version of her life is presented for what would have happened if the doors had closed a split second later, and as a result she does indeed catch both the train and him. Throughout the film the parallel tales are then told of how each development in the heroine's subsequent life unfolds as a result of that initial moment of pure chance. Nothing, the film argues, is inevitable, but rather everything is contingent upon everything else. As André Maurois put it: 'There is no privileged past ... There is an infinity of Pasts, all equally valid ... At each and every instant of Time, however brief you suppose it, the line of events forks like the stem of a tree putting forth twin branches.'

Of course this line of thought infuriates the Whigs, Marxists and Determinists and anyone who believes that some kind of preordained Destiny or Fate or Providence determines human existence. In his tremendously influential book *What Is History?*, the Marxist historian and apologist for Leninism E. H. Carr denounced counterfactual history as a 'red herring' and an 'idle parlour-game'. E. P. Thompson called it something in German that can't be translated for the family readership that hopefully might be buying this book. Eric Hobsbawm is predictably equally dismissive, because Marxism requires humans to operate according to a predetermined dialectical materialism, and not by the caprices of accident or serendipity.

It seems to me that anything that has been condemned by Carr, Thompson *and* Hobsbawm must have something to recommend it, especially if on the other side of the argument we have such distinguished supporters and practitioners of the counterfactual technique as Edward Gibbon, Winston Churchill, Thomas Carlyle, Sir Lewis Namier, Hugh Dacre, Harold Nicolson, Isaiah Berlin, Ronald Knox, Emil Ludwig, G. K. Chesterton, H. A. L. Fisher, Conrad Russell and the utterly delightful Gwyneth Paltrow. (It was Russell who gave us the sobering thought that: 'If we had not invented, during the winter of 1938/39, a new alloy and a new furnace to make it which hardened the propeller casing of the Spitfire, and made it 50 m.p.h. faster than the Messerschmitt instead of 50 m.p.h. slower, it is surely likely that Hitler would have won the war.')

A new book by the former All Souls Fellow Professor Jonathan Clark, entitled *Our Shadowed Present: Modernism, Postmodernism and History*, makes a powerful intellectual case for using the counterfactual tool, albeit of course sparingly, in the study of history. As one of the most profound Tory thinkers in the field of historiography, Professor Clark is adamant that both modernists and postmodernists concentrate far too much on what he calls 'the idolatry of the actual'. In the conclusion of his book he points out that in his own home ground of the 'long' eighteenth century,

[revolutionary] actions that had a considerable chance of success are explained away by a hegemonic ideology, diminished in retrospect to the level of wild gambles, like the French invasion attempt of 1744 or the potentially French-backed Irish rebellion of 1797–8. In both cases, a plan made a domestic rising contingent on foreign military intervention that never materialised; but had the pieces fallen into place, as they did in 1660, 1688 and 1776, the historical landscape could have been transformed.

He goes on:

This aversion from counterfactuals does not abolish their force. Whatever our unthinking preferences for the established certainties and self-evident truths of modernism, or the promised limitless emancipations of postmodernism, counterfactuals implicitly under-pin all historical reconstructions of grand events; only strongly purposeful ideologies condemn the open appraisal of alternatives as disreputable, inspired by an impractical nostalgia.

He is referring, amongst other strongly purposeful ideologies, to Marxism.

Of course, it is pretty rich of the Marxists to denounce the concept of imaginary pasts when it is they who have for over a century and a half now been peddling the most ludicrous of all imaginary futures, one in which the state was somehow going to wither away globally leaving a dictatorship of the very class of people least qualified to exercise power. It is a form of human governance that has never existed any-where – except perhaps for a few months in Barcelona in the Spanish Civil War – because it was based on three ideals – liberty, equality and fraternity – that have time and again been shown to be completely mutually exclusive.

Similarly, the Whig version of history, in which mankind is inexorably moving towards a world of liberal democracy and the Brotherhood of Man, seems to me to be equally deeply flawed. If Germany – perhaps the most culturally civilised and advanced country in the world at the time – could less than a century ago have taken two such sudden and savage steps backwards into barbarism, then surely history, rather than being on the right tracks towards human per-fection, as Macaulay would have us believe, must actually be a locomotive capable of reversing, being shunted into sidings, or even smashing up in a ghastly crash such as that which happened to Germany between 1914 and 1918 and then again from 1933 to 1945.

The Whig and Marxist theories of history should have long ago been replaced by a more believable one, in which What Ifs can play an important role by reminding us that no route is predestined. In this view of the world, Man is a fallen, Originally Sinful being, who strives to do better than previous generations by trying to learn from them, but is ever-conscious of the abysses below, and is as familiar with a knowable past as he is suspicious of plans to get to a necessarily unmappable future utopia.

It was Sir Lewis Namier who said that 'The enduring achievement of historical study is an historical sense – an intuitive understanding – of how things do not happen.' Historians and biographers continually find the most difficult part of their job is to try to remember that their subjects could not possibly have known what was about to happen next, any more than I can accurately predict what will happen at tomorrow's 3.20 at Uttoxeter.

With all our knowledge of the past we can't look one minute into the future, and so it is not really legitimate to feel superior to the actors of the past who had to take their daily decisions not knowing what we know now. The absurdity of Louis XVI on 13 July 1789, as he contemplates with equanimity the next day's hunting at Fontainebleau, seems complete, but only because we know what was about to happen to the Bastille on the fourteenth. Rather than feeling smug about Bourbon idiocy, we ought to be wondering what morons future generations will think of us that we did not realise the mortal danger posed to Western civilisation by mobile phones or space travel or the Jerry Springer Show.

The historian Robert Cowley – one of our contributors in this volume – has argued that in an age which does not know much history, 'Counterfactual speculations can help to awaken and nourish our historical imaginations.' All too often at schools and universities, he believes, 'Students are left with the impression that history is inevitable, that what happened could not have happened any other way. Where in their textbooks are the drama of clashing wills, motives and ideas, of opposing economic and social forces, of accidents and contingencies? . . . A rigorous counterfactual examination has a way of making the stakes of a confrontation or a decision stand out in relief. Too, it can focus on moments that were true turning points.'

Furthermore, if we accept that there is no such thing as historical inevitability and that nothing is preordained, political lethargy – one of the scourges of our day – should be banished, since it means that in human affairs anything is possible. *Che sara, sara* is the philosophy of the wastrel down the ages, and has no place in a world where everything is contingent and circumstantial.

By my desk at home I have a framed letter written by Aldous Huxley in 1959 which says: 'That men do not learn very much from the lessons of history is the most important of all the lessons that history has to teach us.' One advantage of imaginary history is that, properly used, it might be able to teach us new lessons about how to look at the past. It reminds us of the choices that constantly presented themselves to decision-makers in the past, for whom there were an infinite number of possible futures. It reminds us of the role of chance and accident in human affairs. At its best it should also make us eschew hubris, by reminding us what so easily might have been – and what still might be – around only the next corner.

The Cleopatra's Nose theory of history first propounded by Pascal in the seventeenth century, in which the whole history of the Roman Empire would have been different if Cleopatra's nose had been half an inch longer or shorter, is not really admissible. Just as the flapping of a butterfly's wings in the Amazon does not actually cause thunderstorms over the River Trent, and – contrary to Thomas Carlyle's assertions – an Indian does not really alter the globe's centre of gravity when he casts a stone into Lake Ontario, so the workings of cause and effect have to be credible. There were all sorts of other motivations behind the actions of Cæsar and Antony besides sexual attraction for the female pharaoh and, anyhow, for all we know her nose might have been the one thing that neither of them liked about her.

In the enduring philosophical debate between Carlyle's Great Man theory of history and the Determinists' view that it is what T. S. Eliot once called 'vast impersonal forces' – such as industrialisation, materialism, proletarianisation, the rise of science and the decline of magic – that explain history, there is no room for the *reductio ad absurdum* of Pascal's theory. The first rule for What If history-writing should be to keep it as believable as possible. We can untune one string, but not the whole violin.

We must also provide for the counter-counterfactual, whereby the most likely alternative outcome is much the same as the one that actually took place. We can speculate what might have happened if Hitler's parents had never met, but must be prepared for the possibility that someone almost equally cynical and fanatical would have become Chancellor of Germany in the early 1930s, there being no shortage of ambitious fascist politicians around at the time. The historian John Lukacs once wrote of a scenario in which Teddy Roosevelt wins the Republican nomination in 1912, brokers an early end to the First World War, but that does not prevent a second European conflagration from breaking out in the first week of September 1939.

The Duke of Wellington claimed that he despised counterfactual history, commenting on Clausewitz's *On War* that: 'It is useless to speculate upon supposed military movements which were never made, and operations which never took place.' Yet of course it was also he who said of Waterloo: 'I do not think it would have done if I had not been there' – as thought-provoking a What If as any. There are any number of French historians who have posited a Napoleonic victory on the slopes of Mont St Jean. Napoleon himself was tortured by the What If of his winning Waterloo, obsessively going over in his mind what went wrong that terrible Sunday afternoon, and creating an alternative future for himself in which he came to terms with the Allies after the battle and quietly settled down to govern France in peace before finally handing over to the King of Rome. This, though, was by then simply not a credible possible outcome. By 1815 the Great Powers had taken Napoleon's measure, and even had he won that battle he would eventually have succumbed to the half-million-strong Russian and Austrian armies that were mustering against him at the time.

The next rule is to keep it short. As Professor Niall Ferguson points out in his magisterial introduction to *Virtual History* – which stands as the undisputed *Ur*-text of the philosophy behind counterfactual history – the genre lends itself naturally to the essay rather than to the book. The best What If books are those edited by J. C. Squire, Robert Cowley, Jonathan North, Kenneth Macksey, Peter Tsouras and Ferguson himself, which comprise collections of short essays by several different authors. When the conceit is extended across hundreds of pages – as in the case of Richard Dreyfus's *The Two Georges*, in which the American War of Independence never took place, or Harry Harrison's *Stars and Stripes Forever*, in which Britain fought on the side of the Confederacy in the American Civil War – it tends towards overstretch. This is because, just as in a game of billiards one might be able to predict what will happen when ball A hits ball B, and an expert player might be able to see in his mind the effect of ball B hitting C and even perhaps C hitting D, it soon becomes impossible to predict with any degree of accuracy what is likely to happen to balls F, G and H, especially if balls A, B and C are still in play and careering around the table.

Of course, pure fiction is an altogether different area: Robert Harris's *Fatherland* or Kingsley Amis's *Russian Hide-and-Seek*, the latter set in a Soviet-occupied Britain, work very well, as does Keith Roberts's novel *Pavane*, set in an England that was successfully subdued by the Spanish

Armada. Its splendid opening sentence reads: 'On a warm July evening of the year 1588, in the royal palace of Greenwich, a woman lay dying, an assassin's bullet lodged in her abdomen and chest.' (The first chapter of the present book contains Anne Somerset's prognostications for a successful Armada.) Kingsley Amis enjoyed writing What Ifs; his novel *The Alteration* was also set in a Britain which had not undergone the Reformation, in which a choirboy faces the prospect of castration to protect his beautiful singing voice. In a wonderful short essay on the 'Day of Infamy' he has a Japanese fleet going through the Panama Canal in order to shell Manhattan. If you think that sounds unlikely, consider the news published in *Die Zeit* in 2002 that the Kaiser had seriously considered bombarding New York and landing 100,000 troops on the east coast of America, in a kind of massive transatlantic version of *The Riddle of the Sands*.

The difference between a What If and mere science fiction is that it is impermissible for Lenin, say, to have a nuclear bomb, or for Cromwell to be able to deploy the Brown Bess rifle. One can be atavistic, however, and there was once an essay written by a military historian that argued that Wellington's army would have done better to have employed the longbow rather than the musket because the former was, even four centuries after Agincourt, superior in terms of accuracy, stopping-power and rate of fire. Military What Ifs tend to be the best. This is because in order to suspend disbelief it is useful to keep the number of high decision-makers down to the minimum, such as often happens in wartime. It is said that God laughs when men make plans, and since battle plans rarely last much longer than the first shock of attack, war is inherently unpredictable – indeed one rather good book by Robert Sobel about what would have happened if Burgoyne had won at Saratoga is actually entitled *For Want of a Nail*.

No conflict has been more heavily subjected to counter-factual analysis than the Second World War. One publisher,

Greenhill Books, even has a special section of its list devoted to various different outcomes of that struggle. Impressively realistic essays have been written on what would have happened if the BEF had been captured at Dunkirk; if France had fought on in 1940; if Franco had joined the Axis; if Russia had invaded Germany rather than the other way around; if Hitler had invaded the Middle East rather than Russia in 1941; if Bletchley had not produced Ultra decrypts; if Rommel had triumphed at El Alamein; if German scientists had invented the A-bomb; if the U-boats had won the Battle of the Atlantic; if the Normandy landings had been flung back into the sea; if the generals had pulled off the July Plot, and if the bombs had fused over Hiroshima and Nagasaki. Of course there is always the moment when the author steps off into the imaginary future at which research is no longer possible, but these essays are written by historians as distinguished as Sir John Keegan and Richard Overy and few of the scenarios are completely implausible. Generals and occasionally politicians play wargames today; what is that besides a continual examination of possible counterfactuals?

Had the Nazis won the Second World War it is certainly not implausible that they, rather than the Americans, would have won the race to the moon. Wernher von Braun, the German rocket scientist who rose to control the Führer's entire rocket programme, after the war became head of the US space research programme, enthusing President Kennedy about the moon project only days before the latter's assassination in November 1963. Could the Swastika, rather than Old Glory, have been hoisted on the moon in the late 1960s? Might the Sea of Tranquillity instead have been called the Sea of Aryan Superiority? It's not impossible.

Another scenario that is also all too plausible, given his tempestuous life, is that in which Winston Churchill was not there to guide the British nation and Empire in 1940. His eventful life could easily have been cut off at any number of places before the pensionable age at which he became Prime

Minister. Of course it is possible that someone like Halifax or Eden, Amery or even Anderson, Bevin, Attlee or Cripps might have led Britain to victory in the Second World War, but can anyone imagine any of them giving the nation its lion's roar? Cardinal Newman said that he looked in vain for the finger of God in history, but Lord Hailsham believed that Churchill's accession to the premiership on the very day that Hitler unleashed his blitzkrieg in the West was the sole time that he could discern the direct intervention of the Almighty in human affairs. Of course that would admit of determinism, which I cannot do, but we can be almost certain that the course of the war would have been very different in ways we cannot even imagine if Churchill had not been there, whatever the Determinists might argue. Einstein said that God does not play at dice, but what I think Lord Hailsham meant was that by giving Civilisation a fighting chance in May 1940, the Almighty was protecting his handiwork from entering what Churchill called 'a new Dark Age'. It is a romantic and even inspiring notion, but for me the idea of God occasionally tipping the scales in human history is a less credible explanation than the admittedly more prosaic one that Lord Halifax simply didn't want the job and there was no one else of sufficient stature to deny it to Churchill.

Occasionally, as in the well-trodden case of 'What would have happened if Hitler had invaded Britain in 1940', What Ifs can actually question our self-perception as a nation. After the initial six to eight weeks of stout resistance that the Home Guard would have put up, would we have collaborated like the French and the Channel Islanders did, especially when there was no hope of resupply from a neutral America thousands of miles away? The instinctive answer one gives goes to the very heart of what it means to be British.

Equally, those who write off What Ifs as a mere parlour game with no practical application should look at the lengths to which Stalin went to hide the truth about what so nearly happened on Thursday 16 October 1941, a date that some historians, such as Laurence Rees, the Head of BBC History, see as the most important single date of the twentieth century. For it was on that day that Stalin decided not to take the special train he had made ready to get him out of Moscow to beyond the Urals, but instead to stick it out in the capital come what may.

If the news had got out that Stalin had indeed left – as it no doubt would have – there can be little doubt that resistance in Moscow and soon afterwards in the western USSR would have collapsed, leaving the Nazis in control of the whole of European Russia, with the most profound long-term consequences for the rest of the twentieth century and doubtless also for this one. So, after the war, Stalin did everything he could to cover up how close that particular What If had actually come to being realised, and it was only after the fall of the Berlin Wall that the truth could finally be revealed. (An alternative ending to this counterfactual is proposed by Simon Sebag Montefiore in chapter nine.)

America has its own What If that can cause controversy even today. When the economic historian R. W. Fogel asked whether the United States' economy could have thrived in the nineteenth century without railways, he was hailed as a brilliant writer. But when he and others then went on to argue that slavery would have survived as a perfectly viable economic system if it had not been eradicated by the Civil War he was violently lambasted for having gone one What If too far. So in the case of Britain, Russia and America, What Ifs are therefore not just what one historian has described as 'after-dinner history'; instead, the contemplation of what might have happened but did not can actually lay bare the national consciousness of great nations.

Politicians constantly think in terms of counterfactuals, however much they might portentously refuse to answer hypothetical questions. When Neil Kinnock warned the electorate not to grow old or fall ill should the Conservatives win the 1992 general election, he was indulging in a classic What

If. Because politics very often boils down to a question of selecting one option out of several, and one can never know what would have happened if a different route had been chosen, it naturally lends itself to What Ifs. And with every choice made, doors close and opportunities are lost, sometimes for ever. That is what gives them the power to induce nostalgia, regret and even occasionally remorse.

The non-invention of scientific advances rarely makes for good What Ifs. The problem tends to be that, unlike Stalin's fateful decision not to leave Moscow as Hitler's armies closed in, there was no particular historical moment that Sir Isaac Newton (or anyone else) *needed* to discover the laws of gravity, since they still operate whether we understand them or not. If Archimedes had, on leaping out of his bath, slipped on the soap and brained himself, the laws of the displacement of mass would not have altered, although Mrs Archimedes would probably have gone to her grave still puzzled about what her husband could possibly have meant by his last word: 'Eureka!'

Whereas we can with some degree of credibility speculate upon what would have happened if Lee Harvey Oswald had missed his moving target from the Dallas book depository in 1963, we cannot know with the first degree of accuracy the knock-on effects of literary non-events, such as Cervantes' not writing *Don Quixote*.

Characters in What Ifs must act according to their true personalities. There is little point in trying to posit an alternative past in which Hitler gets the atomic bomb because of his decency to his German Jewish scientists, for example, because if he were pro-semitic he wouldn't be Hitler, and therefore he probably wouldn't need a bomb in the first place. As Daniel Snowman put it in his introduction to an excellent book of counterfactual essays: 'If you distort history to the point of giving Alexander Dubček the personality of Marshal Tito, you are back again in the land of whim.'

This is one of the pitfalls skilfully avoided by Snowman in

his book *If I Had Been*, in which he asked ten historians to put themselves in the position of great men of the past and see how they would have, with twenty-twenty hindsight of course, acted differently. Maurice Pearton as Thiers avoids war with Prussia in 1870; Owen Dudley Edwards as Gladstone solves the Irish Question ten years later, and so on. It is an engaging approach to What Ifs, and it works well.

If history teaches us anything about human affairs it is the fatalistic but also faintly reassuring truth that at the end of every triumphal procession there is an open manhole cover. Of course we can never know for certain whether it was left open by accident or by design, but the cock-up theory of history has always seemed to me to be far more plausible than the conspiracy one, not least because of human aptitude: we are even better at cock-ups than we are at conspiracies.

Perhaps the very ubiquity of hubris being punished by nemesis in history should teach us something. One thinks of the slave in ancient Rome who was placed in the victorious general's chariot to whisper in his ear: 'Remember, thou art mortal' as he drove through the cheering crowds during his triumph. He must have been fantastically irritating, but yet how indispensable? Of course, for all we know I might be preordained by an all-powerful kismet or programmed by some kind of false consciousness to write this, but I believe that there is no such thing as historical destiny, for nations any more than for individuals. Fate decrees precisely nothing; there is no grand design in human affairs, simply the multiplied actions of millions of people acting out of a myriad of different motives. God might not play at dice Himself, but at least He permits us to.

The Spanish Armada Lands in England

Anne Somerset

Calling it 'the invincible armada' was not an act of hubris. Also known as 'the most fortunate armada', this great invasion force did indeed meet with every blessing that Providence (aided by the deep purse and careful planning of Philip II) could bestow. It is true that at the outset the venture encountered severe setbacks. In April 1587 Francis Drake's impudent raid on Cadiz delayed the invasion of England by almost a year. Further postponements were caused in February 1588 when the commander of the fleet, the Marquis de Santa Cruz, fell ill, but fortunately his indisposition did not prove fatal. His leadership was crucial to the success of the campaign, for Santa Cruz had been passionate about the 'Enterprise of England' ever since he had first drawn up an invasion plan in 1583. Philip II's respect for his vastly experienced admiral was such that Santa Cruz had even won the right to deviate from the King's written instructions if he judged it appropriate.

On 21 July 1588 the Armada finally sailed for England. The Spaniards were sighted off the Scilly Isles on 29 July and two days later had their first inconclusive encounter with the English fleet. Little damage was done to the ships of either side, but on 1 August the English suffered a major disaster.

When darkness fell on 31 July it had been agreed that the English Vice Admiral Francis Drake should lead the fleet as it pursued the Armada up the Channel. The ships were to be guided by the light of the lantern on the stern of Drake's ship, the *Revenge*. However, when Drake heard that the Spanish vessel *Nuestra Señora del Rosario* had been disabled in an accident, he betrayed the true instincts of a pirate. Extinguishing his lantern, he doubled back past the English fleet and next morning at dawn took possession of the helpless Spanish ship.

Meanwhile, Lord Admiral Howard had been perplexed when he had lost sight of Drake's lantern. A little later he had seen another light, which he assumed was Drake's, and had hastened to catch up with it. The next morning he discovered to his horror that he had strayed into the very midst of the enemy fleet. He had made the fatal mistake of entering the 'horns' of the Armada's crescent formation, depriving him of the wind which would have given him the manoeuvrability to escape. He was promptly grappled by the *San Salvador*, one of the most heavily armed ships in the Spanish fleet. Seeing that Howard was in difficulty, the English ships the *Bear* and the *Mary Rose* came up to assist, with the result that they too were grappled and boarded. After fierce fighting on the decks, the Spaniards gained possession of all three vessels.

The loss of their flagship was a catastrophe from which the English never really recovered. When Drake rejoined the fleet, he was vilified for the inexcusable way he had endangered his country for the sake of gaining plunder. The bitterness and dissension to which the incident gave rise has been blamed for the subsequent failure to formulate a coherent strategy against the enemy.

On 4 August the English suffered another disaster when the largest vessel in the fleet, Martin Frobisher's *Triumph*, was captured by the Spanish. During the night, the ship had been carried forward by the tide so that it had become separated from the main body of the fleet. When dawn broke the *Triumph* found herself isolated and becalmed near the Spanish fleet. The Spaniards promptly attacked, and though Frobisher made desperate efforts to escape by ordering small boats powered by oars to tow his stranded ship, all proved in vain. Once the Spaniards had approached near enough to grapple, the *Triumph*'s seizure was inevitable.

Cheered by these successes, the Armada continued its stately progress up the Channel. The English were unable to inflict any significant damage on the enemy and were taken aback on the evening of 6 August when the Spaniards suddenly anchored before Calais. Having stopped there, Santa Cruz established contact with the town's governor, a fervent member of the Catholic League who was in the pay of Don Bernardino de Mendoza, the Spanish ambassador to France. As well as providing the Spanish with fresh victuals and water, the governor performed an invaluable service by replenishing the Armada's depleted ammunition stocks. At that point the Spaniards' supplies of smaller-calibre cannon balls were near to exhaustion, but this vital aid renewed the fleet's offensive capacity.

In desperation the English attempted to send fireships among the Spanish fleet on the night of 7 August, but the manoeuvre failed because there was little wind to propel the eight unmanned vessels. In consequence they moved so sluggishly that Spanish pinnaces succeeded in intercepting them. Having been diverted from their target, the fireships were towed away and then left to run aground on the French coast.

On 1 August Santa Cruz had sent a ship bearing a message to the Duke of Parma, Philip II's commander in the Netherlands, that the Armada was approaching. Declaring that it was time to synchronise their operations, he had urged the Duke to launch without delay his fleet of flat-bottomed barges that were to carry his troops from Dunkirk and Nieuport to England. The message reached Parma on 6 August, and he at once activated his embarkation plan. By an amazing feat of logistics, all of Parma's 17,000 men were aboard their craft within thirty-six hours. A squadron of English ships under Henry Seymour had been patrolling the waters off Dunkirk with orders to attack Parma if he put to sea. On 6 August, however, these ships had rejoined the main English fleet in order to assist it in the struggle against the Armada. It had been assumed that the flyboats of the Dutch navy could be relied upon to keep Parma bottled up in port, but this proved to be a disastrous error.

Despite the fact that the outlook for them was bleak if the English were defeated, the Dutch were currently on very bad terms with their English allies. They had been infuriated by Queen Elizabeth's insistence on continuing peace nego-tiations with the Duke of Parma right up to the moment when the Armada began sailing up the Channel. They sus-pected that the Queen was planning to make a separate peace which took no account of their interests, and this had resulted in a complete breakdown of trust between the two powers. Misleading intelligence reports had convinced the Dutch that the army Parma had gathered together was intended for an invasion of Holland and Zealand and that the Armada was planning to seize Ostend or another port in Dutch possession. As a result England was left open to attack while the Dutch ranged their forces to protect their own coast from a threat that never materialised.

When formulating his invasion plan Philip II had expressed the confident belief that, since God knew that the venture was dedicated to His service, He would favour it with His blessing. The King's faith in the Almighty proved justified: when Parma's flotilla of barges emerged from their havens at dawn on 8 August conditions for the crossing could not have been more perfect. A light breeze sped the boats on their way without whipping up the waves.

Despite the fact that communication between them had been so limited, the movements of Parma's army and the Spanish fleet were perfectly co-ordinated. Shortly after Parma's forces had set off on their voyage to England, Santa Cruz's ships came out from Calais. With the wind in their favour, they engaged the English fleet in battle. For the next nine hours a vicious fire-fight raged. Although ships in both fleets were badly battered, neither side succeeded in gaining the advantage over the other. The English had hoped that their superior firepower would give them the edge in an engagement, but the Spanish fired back so fiercely that the English were unable to sail close enough to inflict serious damage. When Francis Drake tried to bring his ship nearer to the enemy, he was fatally wounded by a musket shot. By late afternoon both sides had exhausted their ammunition. Taking advantage of another change in the wind, the Spanish fleet now sailed northward. The English navy followed them, unaware that while they had been battling their opponents, Parma had crossed the narrow seas and landed in England.

On 12 August the Armada entered the Firth of Forth and anchored off Leith. Having run out of victuals, the English fleet was compelled to leave the enemy there and return to home ports. Once James VI of Scotland heard that Parma's army had landed in England, he judged it prudent to give the Spaniards a friendly reception. Declaring himself delighted by the opportunity to exact revenge on the Jezebel who had murdered his mother, he agreed that Santa Cruz's ships could remain in harbour to perform repairs and take on more water.

Meanwhile, to the south Parma was sweeping all before him. The sea crossing had taken less than eight hours, and on the afternoon of 8 August Parma's barges had landed unopposed at Margate. As these boats had made their way to England the flotilla had been joined by a few ships which Santa Cruz had ordered to separate from the main body of the Armada. Besides carrying soldiers to reinforce Parma's army, these vessels contained equipment such as wheeled cannon which could be transported overland. The English had predicted that Parma would land in Essex, and the bulk of the Queen's forces had therefore been concentrated there. Kent had been left virtually undefended with only 4,000 inexperienced men being scattered about the county. The news that Parma had landed prompted mass desertions, and the rump that remained at their posts were incapable of offering serious resistance to troops who were acknowledged to be 'the best soldiers at this day in Christendom'.

Within a week Parma had reached London. He had

followed the route taken by Wyatt's rebels more than thirty years before, crossing the Thames at Kingston and then marching on the capital. Anticipating that the Spaniards would approach from the east, the Queen had planned to withdraw to Windsor Castle if it appeared that London was in danger of falling. The rapid enemy advance from the opposite direction cut off her escape route and prevented her from reaching this easily defensible stronghold.

In late June Lord Admiral Howard had prophesied that if the Spaniards succeeded in gaining a foothold in England it would 'breed great danger'. This warning proved all too accurate. The Queen had made matters worse for herself by choosing the Earl of Leicester as the commander of her army, despite the fact that his military record was undistinguished. When confronted by this latest challenge, he displayed his usual incompetence. Since he died of natural causes only three weeks after the Spaniards gained London, it is probable that he was already mortally ill, and that this had impaired his judgement.

On 8 August, when the Spaniards first set foot in England, Leicester was still assembling his army at Tilbury in Essex. No more than 8,000 men had gathered there by that date, but Leicester was finding it difficult to provide even for these modest numbers. Shortage of food was so acute that Leicester had been obliged to send some of the men back to their counties. In the course of the coming week thousands more were expected to arrive at Tilbury, but it was unclear if by that time arrangements would be in place to feed them.

The news that the enemy had landed caused panic in the camp at Tilbury. Many of those serving there felt unequal to the challenge of taking on Parma's seasoned veterans and from the start a mood of defeatism was evident. With hindsight it is clear that the English had placed too much reliance on the protection afforded them by their navy, and that land defences had been given insufficient attention.

In theory, county militias had met regularly during the

past year to conduct martial exercises and to handle their weapons, but reality had fallen far short of this. There had been widespread absenteeism, and even those who had been most eager to acquire a military training had been hampered by disorganisation and a lack of equipment. In 1588 the men who joined Leicester's army from the counties were meant to bring weapons with them, but frequently they had not been issued with any and so arrived empty-handed. Others came bearing only bows and arrows, which were no match for the more modern armaments carried by the Spaniards. Worse still, many of these putative archers had never attended target practice, and thus had not even mastered this outdated technology. To complete the shambles, those who had been given firearms often lacked ammunition. Attempts to remedy these deficiencies by distributing munitions stored in the Tower of London failed to make up the shortfall.

On learning that Parma's troops were advancing through Kent, Leicester sought vainly to reposition his army. A pontoon bridge was supposed to have been erected over the Thames so that the army could cross from Tilbury to Gravesend, but the structure was still unusable. Leicester wasted valuable time trying to complete it before finally acknowledging that the effort was futile. The Spaniards were making such rapid progress that it was clear that by the time the English army had been transferred to the opposite bank of the Thames, it would be too late to intercept the enemy. Instead Leicester decided to join his army with the troops gathered in London for the protection of the Queen's person under the command of Lord Hunsdon. If anything, however, this unexpected influx of armed men into the capital only added to the sense of chaos and confusion.

On 16 August the Spanish army surged into London. The chains that had been slung across some streets in a bid to obstruct them proved little impediment to their advance. Fearing that their city would be sacked, Londoners were paralysed with terror, and the army which was meant to repulse an attack scarcely proved more resolute. Some of its leaders fought bravely and Lords Hunsdon and Essex were both killed in hand-to-hand combat with the enemy, but their troops were soon overwhelmed by the Spaniards' determined onslaught. Casualties on the Spanish side were remarkably light, while English losses were estimated at one thousand.

Before long St James's Palace was surrounded. Acknowledging that the situation was hopeless, the Queen offered to surrender in order to avoid further bloodshed. The Spaniards confined her in her chamber and the following day issued an announcement that she had died in her sleep. In reality she had been strangled by her captors. When the news was conveyed to Philip II in Spain he was seen to chuckle, commenting that he was delighted that 'God has rid us of the Englishwoman'. He added that it made him shudder to think that had she accepted his proposal, they would have been man and wife for the past thirty years.

As the Spaniards had calculated, Elizabeth's removal made their task much easier. While there was widespread sadness at her fate (for the claim that she had met a peaceful end was universally disbelieved), most of her former subjects concluded that now that the Queen was dead, further defiance was pointless. Elizabeth had left no designated successor around whom resistance could coalesce, and in the absence of such a figurehead the will to fight on crumbled.

Having taken possession of the kingdom, the Spaniards wasted no time in starting its reconversion to Catholicism. As soon as the capital was secured, Cardinal William Allen was shipped over from Flanders and named as Archbishop of Canterbury. All over the country Jesuits and priests emerged from hiding-holes located within the houses of Catholic gentry, and their numbers were soon reinforced when they were joined by the 180 priests who had sailed aboard the Armada. In September a victory parade was followed by a thanksgiving mass at St Paul's, for which William Byrd composed a particularly fine anthem.

Reconversion was accompanied by repression. Since Parma was anxious to return to the Netherlands, Philip named Mendoza as Governor General of England. When he had been expelled from the country in 1584 for fomenting rebellion, Mendoza had declared that he was 'born not to disturb kingdoms but to conquer them'. With his triumphant return this boast was vindicated. Mendoza set up 'the council of resettlement', swiftly rechristened 'the bloody tribunal'. Pending the establishment of the Inquisition, this body was authorised to try cases of heresy as well as political offences. In November a great *auto-da-fé* was held at Smithfield. Among those burnt was Elizabeth's last Archbishop of Canterbury, John Whitgift, who perished alongside some of the Puritan ministers he had formerly persecuted. Another eminent victim was former Secretary of State Sir Francis Walsingham, who died accusing his late mistress of having betrayed the Protestant cause in hopes of conserving her treasure.

Shortly afterwards Lord Burghley was beheaded on Tower Hill for having committed treason against his rightful monarch Mary Stuart. Other councillors of the Queen, such as Sir Christopher Hatton, had their estates confiscated. The proceeds from some of these forfeitures were used to set up new monasteries, but the monastic revival did not progress very far. The nunneries established at the same time proved more popular with noble families who welcomed the opportunity to settle unmarried daughters in these institutions.

In contrast to what had happened in the reign of Mary Tudor, English Protestants were unable to seek refuge abroad. Some attempted to practise their religion in secret, but spies and informers soon penetrated the underground Puritan network, and its members were tried as heretics. No mercy was shown to those who refused to relinquish their faith. In the ten years that followed the conquest of England, the Holy Inquisition executed more than three thousand individuals, the majority coming from the educated classes. In some ways, however, it proved remarkably easy to undo the effects of the English Reformation. The persecution of heretics was deeply unpopular, but when faced with a choice between conformity and death, most people opted to convert.

To keep the populace quiescent, an army of occupation remained in the country for several years, and soldiers were billeted in private households. Shortly after his arrival, Mendoza announced that the English must compensate the Spaniards for losses incurred as a result of Drake's depredations and for having supported the rebels in the Netherlands. A sales tax of ten per cent on all goods was introduced, despite protests from the mercantile community that this would be ruinous for trade. The imposition raised enormous sums, and permanently secured the Crown an independent source of revenue.

The repercussions of the Spanish triumph were felt all over Europe. Following their victory the Spaniards regained possession of Flushing and Brill, the cautionary towns which had been handed over to Elizabeth before she sent an army to the Netherlands. This made it impossible for the Dutch to continue their struggle against their Spanish overlords. Within months the Dutch had had to offer their unconditional surrender. Protestantism was outlawed throughout the Netherlands and a new constitution abrogating their traditional laws and liberties was imposed on the United Provinces.

In France Henry III remained in subjection to the Catholic League and their pro-Spanish leader, the Duke of Guise. The King was forced to disinherit the Protestant Henry of Navarre, and for the next ten years real power resided with Guise. During that time France was effectively a client state of Spain, but by the time Philip II died in 1598 tensions were evident between the two countries. The Duke of Guise was scheming to have himself declared Henry III's successor, whereas King Philip favoured the claims of his daughter Catalina, who was married to the Duke of Savoy.

James VI of Scotland converted to Catholicism in 1589. Thereafter he was careful to remain on good terms with his powerful neighbours in England. Having broken off his engagement to Anne of Denmark, he suggested to King Philip that he should become the husband of the Infanta Isabella. The proposal was rejected with contempt and in the end James married an illegitimate daughter of the Duke of Parma.

Spanish foreign policy had triumphed at every turn, but Philip II was not satisfied with these achievements. He spent the last months of his life planning a great crusade against the Turks. Simultaneously he was pressuring his Habsburg cousins to rescind the Augsburg Settlement and outlaw Protestantism throughout the empire, a move guaranteed to plunge Germany into chaos.

At his death Philip II effectively dominated all Europe, but following his victory in 1588 he had decided against making himself England's titular ruler. Dreading the prospect of revisiting a country he had loathed when he had gone there as Mary Tudor's husband, Philip had instead proclaimed his daughter Isabella Queen of England. In 1590 the state of emergency in England was declared at an end and Isabella and her new husband, Archduke Albert, arrived to take up the reins of government. The couple soon became personally popular and helped reconcile the English to their occupation by a foreign power. Isabella and Albert endeared themselves to the country by their willingness to seek advice from their Privy Council, composed of members of the old Catholic nobility such as the Earl of Westmoreland (newly returned from exile) and Lord Henry Howard. In 1592 Parliament met again for the first time since the conquest. The assembly's powers were much reduced because the Crown no longer derived a significant portion of its income from parliamentary grants. Nevertheless the fact that it had been permitted to convene did at least provide the English with a forum to articulate grievances and gave them some hope that their rights would one day be restored.

Isabella and her husband were enthusiastic proponents of colonisation. With their encouragement Raleigh's former colony in Virginia (renamed Sainted Virgin) was resettled and was soon prospering. Within years, however, the colonists were complaining that they were subjected to excessive bureaucratic regulation and restrictions on commerce. The resentment this caused foreshadowed their secession from the mother country which took place two centuries later.

As England grew accustomed to its new rulers, it experienced a cultural revival. In the mid 1590s plays by William Shakespeare were first staged at the Rose Theatre. Over the next fifteen years his output was prolific, with his magisterial cycle of history plays being among his best productions. Perhaps his most memorable creation was the villainous protagonist of his 1597 play, *Henry VII*. This monster of avarice revels in his evil deeds but does not lack sardonic humour. The dramatic climax of the play comes when the usurper browbeats Elizabeth of York into accepting his hand in marriage immediately after he has arranged for her brothers, the Princes in the Tower, to be murdered.

The cycle of history plays was brought to a close with Shakespeare's last great work, *Henry VIII*. Its most powerful scene occurs at the christening of the infant Elizabeth when the wronged Catherine of Aragon bursts into the chapel to harangue King Henry. Having excoriated Anne Boleyn as a heretic and whore, she points at the child in the font and declares that England will be cast into darkness if this bastard ascends the throne. Only with the accession of a true heir of the house of Lancaster will the nation's sufferings be ended.

The flowering of this native genius is indicative of the gradual rebuilding of self-confidence which took place as the English recovered from the shattering experience of military defeat and came to terms with their lost autonomy. As well as being one of the undisputed glories of the Isabelline age, the plays helped the English to preserve a distinctive sense of their own identity. Having provided his countrymen with a glorious national heritage, Shakespeare was hugely influential in shaping their vision of the past.

The Gunpowder Plot Succeeds

Antonia Fraser

The coronation of Queen Elizabeth II took place on a fine, fair day in January 1606 – the fifteenth to be precise, in honour of her glorious predecessor, the first Elizabeth, who had been crowned on that very day in 1559. This was not the only deliberate echo of that previous sacred festivity. Elizabeth I, who once said that 'In pompous ceremonies a secret of government doth much consist, for that the people are both naturally taken and help with exterior shows', would have understood the reasoning. At the same time she would have utterly abhorred the circumstances which had brought about this new coronation, less than three years after the accession to the throne of Elizabeth II's father, James I.

So the young Elizabeth Stuart, eldest daughter of James and his Danish Queen Anne, had spent three nights before her coronation in the Tower as was customary for sovereigns, and as her father (and the great Elizabeth) had done in their time. She had then processed to Westminster Abbey through streets with fresh gravel flung down, where the windows were hung with banners. A canopy was carried over her head and an enormous mantle made from twenty-five yards of gold and silver tissue was wrapped around her. At the age of nine and a half, Elizabeth II might have been in danger of being dwarfed by her imposing surroundings. Fortunately she was tall for her age (taking after her late mother, or perhaps her grandmother Mary Queen of Scots), her appearance further enhanced by the dignity of her bearing, on which all commented. Elizabeth II was already showing signs of great beauty with her huge heavy-lidded hazel eyes and her delicate oval face; that was something which certainly excited the French ambassador. He was not used to a matrimonial prize such as this unmarried queen being so 'very well bred and handsome', in his own words.

The other aspect of the new queen's appearance noted by all the spectators both along the route and in the Abbey itself – but not mentioned publicly – was her extraordinary air of melancholy. It did not pass during the crowning itself, when it was as though the actual crown was weighing her head down; and it did not pass when the Lord Protector Henry Percy, Earl of Northumberland, escorted her back down the aisle of the Abbey. Yet her composure remained complete; it was with an air of philosophic sadness rather than tempestuous grief that Elizabeth II accepted her destiny. She showed only one moment of animation, although so fleeting that many missed it, and that was in response to a shout from someone in the crowd outside the Abbey. Instead of the huzzas, the cheers and the 'Vivat Elizabethas' so carefully orchestrated by the new government, a voice had the temerity to call out: 'Long live the Protestant king over the border, long live King Charles.' Perhaps a tear shone in the new queen's eye. But Elizabeth II quickly recovered her melancholy composure; there was a scuffle and the audacious dissenter was dragged away by soldiers. The usual penalties for anti-government protest, the stocks and mutilation of the ears, were no doubt exacted.

The tragic air of Elizabeth Stuart, Queen of Great Britain, was hardly to be wondered at. For this scenario of her accession and coronation proposes that her father, mother and elder brother Henry Prince of Wales, as well as the preponderance of the nobility, higher clergy and many members of the House of Commons had died in a colossal explosion at the Opening of Parliament less than three months before, on 5 November 1605. Elizabeth, at the house of her governor the Lord Harington, Coombe Abbey in the Midlands near Rugby, had escaped the blast.

Of the surviving members of what had once been the

most flourishing young royal family in recent British history, Elizabeth's younger sister Princess Mary, seven months old at the time of the disaster, was a delicate child who would in fact shortly succumb to one of the many common infant illnesses. Then there was Prince Charles, recently created Duke of York, the usual title of the king's second son: undersized, a late walker and talker, he was not yet five at the time of the explosion. Prince Charles had not in the end been at the Opening of Parliament, although the possibility had been discussed. He had been considered too young and, frankly, too lacking in the kind of glamour which princes and princesses were supposed to display to impress the people with their favourite 'exterior shows'. It was Charles's elder brother Henry Prince of Wales whose appearance, tall, handsome and martial, had incarnated everything a nation might hope for in its future ruler. Charles on the other hand was believed to be such a liability that he had only been brought down from Scotland to join his brother and sisters in late 1604, and then courtiers had not rushed to join the new royal household for fear the puny little prince would die and leave them stranded.

How ironic it was, then, that of King James's 'cubs' as he proudly called them, boasting happily of the royal nursery which the late Virgin Queen had never been able to provide, it was the despised Charles who had survived the blast, and that because of his own weakness. After that, Charles's destiny was to be strange indeed: rescued by loyal Scottish servants from the mayhem of Westminster, he was rushed north to the safety of Scotland and there proclaimed king by the Scottish nobles, who were only too anxious to recover the independence they had so recently lost with the accession of their king to the mightier English throne.

In January 1606, in the immediate aftermath of the successful Gunpowder Plot, there were thus two sovereigns within the British Isles: one, nominally Catholic, at any rate heavily supported by Catholic France, Elizabeth II; the other, nominally Protestant or rather Calvinist, Charles I, upheld in Scotland and upheld by the Scottish nobility – for the time being without foreign support.

The Plot had its genesis in the despair in the hearts of the Catholic community after the new king, James I, had – in their view – broken the promises he made to them while in Scotland. The persecution of Catholics, involving fines, imprisonments, barbarously carried-out deaths of priests, deaths for those who harboured priests, had been horribly severe in the last years of Elizabeth I's reign. The Mass itself was an illegal act, and the various other disabilities imposed upon Catholics for even the discreet practice of their religion make harrowing reading. It was on the Catholics that all men fastened their hatred, wrote a priest who was himself imprisoned in the Tower, Father William Weston: 'They lay in ambush for them, betrayed them, attacked them with violence and without warning. They plundered them at night, confiscated their possessions, drove away their flocks, stole their cattle.' In a way even more harrowing to devout Catholics was the fact that they were not allowed to baptise their children Catholics but were compelled to do so in a Protestant church, just as adults had to marry in a Protestant church. Protestant churchgoing on Sundays was also compulsory for fear of fines.

All this meant that the Catholic recusant population – the word comes from refusal, the refusal of Catholics to attend Protestant services – had largely gone underground by the time Elizabeth I died. The head of the family and his male heir might profess the Protestant faith, to avoid fines and loss of properties, while the rest of the family, especially the mother, remained Catholic, carrying the torch forward to future generations in secret. In general the Catholic women took advantage of their presumed weakness and virtually non-existent status at law, to protect priests and generally preserve the network of the faithful. People turned Catholic on their deathbeds when it could no longer damage them materially, having probably been Catholic in their hearts all along.

It was therefore especially significant in terms of the Gunpowder Plot (and its possible success) that no one really knew for sure, nor could know, how many Catholics there were in England in 1603 and whether their numbers would remain static in the months that followed. The Anglican bishops assured their new king at his accession that there were only 8,000 recusant adults, whereas it has been suggested that the true figure was more like 35,000. Three years later this figure was said to have risen to 100,000 under the comparatively mild regime with which James started – something which fatally aroused Catholic hopes before dashing them again with severer penalties. (As a contemporary percipiently observed of the Gunpowder Plot, 'hope deferred maketh the heart sick'.)

This emergence of the Catholics from the shadows did not pass without comment – hostile comment. In the words of Sir Henry Spiller in a speech in Parliament, 'The strength of the Catholic body, with the suspension of persecution, at once became evident.' Yet the idea of 65,000 adults becoming suddenly convinced of the truth of Catholic religion in a short space of time is evidently ludicrous. The true picture is of a large if unquantifiable body of people ready and willing to worship according to the faith of their Catholic ancestors, provided they could do so with impunity for their families and their properties. King James, following the (real-life) failure of the Plot, referred to the conspirators' vain hopes of a 'snowball' effect: they had been 'dreaming to themselves that they had the virtues of a snowball' which would begin in a small way, but by 'tumbling down from a great hill' would grow to an enormous size, 'gathering snow all the way'. But it was the fire of failure which melted the snowball; victory would surely have produced a very different result, with Catholics in large numbers coming out.

The basic elements of the Gunpowder Plot were as follows: a soldier of fortune named Guy Fawkes, a Catholic who had been serving in the (Spanish-ruled) Netherlands for some time and had indeed adopted the foreign version of his name, Guido, was brought back into his native country. This was for the purpose of placing an enormous quantity of gunpowder in the so-called 'cellar' of the House of Lords. The cellar was in fact on the ground floor rather than underground (as generations of myths about Fawkes as the sinister mole-in-the-black-vault would go on to pretend). Used sometimes for the coal and firewood needed for heating and cooking, it had also accrued over the years detritus such as pieces of masonry and was in general untidy and very dirty: in fact more of a storehouse than a cellar.

The cellar belonged to the house of one John Whynniard which lay conveniently enough right in the heart of Westminster, at right angles to the House of Lords, parallel to a short passage which was known as Parliament Place. This led on to Parliament Stairs, which gave access to the river some forty yards away. The cellar itself happened to be directly under the chamber of the House of Lords where the Opening of Parliament was always held. It was rented in advance – without any difficulty at all – by one of the chief conspirators. This was Thomas Percy, a kinsman of the powerful Earl of Northumberland who had been involved in Catholic intrigues even before the accession of James I to the throne.

One should emphasise, odd as it may seem to a highly security-conscious age like our own, especially where the seat of government is concerned, that there was nothing at all odd about this rental; Thomas Percy simply explained that he needed additional accommodation for his servant with his wife in London, paid his £4 rental and that was that. Nor was the potentially lethal position of the cellar itself a problem. The Palace of Westminster, at this date and for many years to come, was a warren of meeting-rooms, semi-private chambers and apartments as well as commercial enterprises of all sorts (as the diaries of Pepys sixty years later amply attest). Still less did the inhabitants of Westminster show any signs of recognising the servant 'John Johnson' for what he was: a Catholic conspirator under an assumed identity. Fawkes had been abroad for some years and although the busy government intelligence service had his actual name in their sights, the connection was never made (in real life) until Fawkes himself confessed under torture.

Providing the gunpowder, at this period, was not a problem either, another pertinent if surprising fact. The government in theory had the monopoly but it meant little in practical terms when gunpowder was part of the equipment of every soldier, including the militia and trained bands, and every merchant vessel had a substantial stock. Proclamations from the government forbidding the selling-off of ordnance and munitions, including gunpowder, show how common the practice was. A total of thirty-six barrels were acquired without difficulty and introduced into the cellar by the easy river route. This was the common means of communication between the two banks of the Thames at this time, the chief conspirator Robert Catesby having his lodgings on the south side of the river. Although estimates of the amount of gunpowder have differed due to the many unreliable testimonies which followed the (real-life) dénouement, 10,000 pounds is the highest figure and 2,000 the lowest; no one has ever disputed that this was more than enough to blow the House of Lords and its wretched denizens sky-high.

A conveniently placed cellar, a huge quantity of explosive, an obscure conspirator ready to touch the fuse and then escape by the river: all these elements were well and truly in place in November 1605 with no particular reason why they should have been discovered before the big bang itself took place – had it not been for treachery by an insider. But of course no conspiracy of this sort exists in a vacuum and it was the motivation which was the crucial element here, bringing with it many complications including natural human resistance to the shedding of blood of innocent people for some higher cause.

The charismatic leader Robert Catesby, who had called his companions to a meeting in a London tavern in May 1604 with the words 'The nature of the disease requires so sharp a remedy', was by now in the Midlands. In Warwickshire and elsewhere – Shakespeare's country, remembering Shakespeare's own strong recusant origins – Catholic feeling had never been suppressed. It was probably the fine young horseman Sir Everard Digby, a familiar figure at the court, who was deputed to seize the Princess Elizabeth before proclaiming her queen and it was almost certainly the Earl of Northumberland who was intended to act as her regent or Protector during her childhood.

Although nothing of this nature was ever proved against Northumberland and he was actually among those peers who attended the Opening of Parliament, it was not for nothing that he was imprisoned subsequently in the Tower of London. Logic told the government that the conspirators must have had a prominent figure in mind to lead the regime in the name of Elizabeth (as Protector Somerset had done for the nine-year-old Edward VI). On the night of 4 November Northumberland, at his base near London at Syon House, suddenly announced that he was 'sleepy because of his early rising that day' and would not attend. It is true that this spasm of fatigue – if it was fatigue and not self-preservation – passed; but the fact that Northumberland changed his mind yet again and did attend may have been due to someone tipping him off that (in real life) the gunpowder had been discovered in the vaults and removed . . . in which case Northumberland needed to act quickly in order to establish his innocence.

So far there was nothing in the Plot itself which guaranteed failure – and with its sheer daring, there was a great hope of a triumphant if gruesome success. The human element which led to the discovery a few days in advance of the intended explosion was the mixed reaction of Lord Monteagle to the news of what was intended. He was probably informed of what was planned by one of the conspirators, his brother-in-law Francis Tresham. Monteagle on the one hand revolted at the thought of the deaths of the innocent and on the other hand saw a splendid opportunity for personal advancement by warning the Chief Minister Salisbury (and the King) of what was threatening. There have been many proposed explanations of the anonymous Monteagle Letter, which was delivered in a suitably mysterious fashion under cover of darkness. It began: 'My Lord ... devise some excuse to shift of your attendance at this Parliament ... For though there be no appearance of any stir, yet I say they shall receive a terrible blow this Parliament and yet they shall not see who hurts them ...'. However, the obvious theory, that Monteagle wrote it himself, is not easily contradicted, since he was the enormous beneficiary of the whole business. If Monteagle had not succumbed to the temptation of treachery for a mixture of motives, noble and material, there is no reason to suppose that the Plot would have been detected in advance.

Let us suppose, then, that the Gunpowder Plot, with its avowed aim of ending the persecution of the Catholics, is successful in nearly all its elements – with one tiny failure or rather bungle, seemingly unimportant in the general confusion (and conspiratorial rejoicing) but with, it is suggested, momentous consequences. The plotters had never really grappled with the question of little Prince Charles, the runt of the litter who had arrived so late on the royal family scene. After assuming that he would attend the House of Lords like his elder brother, they had vaguely considered abducting him if he didn't. Subsequent to the discovery of the Plot one of Prince Charles's servants deposed that Thomas Percy had come to the little Prince's lodgings and 'made enquiries as to the way into his chamber' and 'where he rode abroad' and with how many attendants. What Percy might have contemplated could, however, easily have been carried out in the immediate aftermath of the explosion by some of the many loyal Scots who had come south with the Prince's father.

The notion of Prince Charles being proclaimed King of Scotland (he was after all by royal rules the rightful heir after the deaths of James and Henry, as a male having precedence over his older sister) and educated as a Calvinist as James had been with stern tutors, is perfectly plausible. His childhood would indeed have had remarkable parallels with that of the young James, ruler from an even younger age, with a series of regents. Many royal children in history had to endure new religious orientations which may have been originally unwelcome (although at under five, and being backward, Charles would not have suffered as much as Elizabeth, already at nine publicly pious as well as Protestant).

I shall return to the question of how the future of King Charles I of Scotland and Queen Elizabeth II of England might have worked out in the years to come. But in the meantime what of England? It is now that the issue of foreign support or the lack of it becomes crucial. The two most powerful European countries – France and Spain – were both Catholic, Henri IV King of France having converted from Protestantism twelve years earlier in order to ascend the throne, with the celebrated quip: 'Paris is worth a Mass'. Spain in addition ruled the so-called Spanish Netherlands, an area that very roughly approximated to modern Belgium, in the persons of the joint Governors, the 'Archdukes' as the married couple were known, Albert and Isabella, respectively nephew and daughter of the King of Spain.

Although in real life all the Catholic powers, including the Pope himself, hastened to express absolute horror at the devilish conspiracy which had been planned, a different result might have brought very different reactions. Northumberland's regime (he was not technically a Catholic, although obviously had strong Catholic sympathies) might have concentrated on binding manifest wounds. With the spirit of the shared religious past invoked he might have attempted to unite loyal Anglicans and Catholics, with persecution for the latter of course ended. (Puritans would have been another matter and would surely have looked yearningly towards Scotland.) Under the circumstances Spain, which had actually cooled on supporting yet another attempt at invasion on behalf of the English Catholics, taking part in a treaty with James I in 1604, might have discovered very different sympathies in the interests of realpolitik. Spain would certainly not have contemplated an invasion on behalf of the English Protestant interest and it may be that the supportive troops from Spanish Flanders, on which the conspirators (remembering Guy Fawkes had served there) pinned such hopes, would actually have arrived.

Still less would the France of the ultra-pragmatic Henri IV have refrained from trying to win the new game of alliances. The researches of John Bossy have shown that around the turn of the seventeenth century, France took a new interest in the plight of the English Catholics, attempting (not with total success) to sort the internal disputes between the Jesuits and the so-called Appellants, priests who were more accommodating with the civil order. There were connections there already and it is difficult to believe that Henri IV would not have played the game to the top of its bent.

At quite a different level, that of matrimonial alliances, one of the French princes was an obvious husband for the new Queen Elizabeth, since the question of Henri's eldest son and the then princess had already been discussed favourably in the lifetime of her father. James had boasted to the French ambassador that his 'Bessy' was already quite enamoured of the Dauphin's portrait. (Elizabeth II, in her revolutionised new life, would at least have been able to comfort herself with that memory.) There had also been some question of a double marriage, despite the difference in religion, with Prince Henry marrying the eldest daughter of France; during his brief lifetime Henry had promised his beloved sister that he would not consent to this unless she duly became Dauphiness. Marie de Médicis and Henri IV had three sons in all, and if marrying the Dauphin (the future Louis XIII) to the Queen of England was now considered altogether too ambitious a project, a combination of the two thrones likely to enrage European opinion, then the conventional route would be to marry a younger French prince to Elizabeth II (as the Duc d'Alençon had been suggested as a bridegroom for her great predecessor).

While this prospect of an Anglo-French closeness is merely sketched in, it would be a conciliatory and practical route for the new government to take. France (and Henri IV) had plenty of understanding of the problem of religious minorities with its sizeable Huguenot population, to which Henri had once belonged. All of this is to suggest that the frightful atrocity – as it would have been – of an explosion killing off most of the English Establishment would not in fact have resulted in a foreign invasion. After all, who would have invaded and to what end? On the contrary, the great powers, as great powers always have, would have searched for an accommodation which was to their own advantage.

It remains to hope that the imaginary reign of Queen Elizabeth II would have been marked by more tolerance towards the Puritan dissident sects than that of the first Elizabeth towards the Catholics. Certainly the young Elizabeth Stuart would have made an excellent queen, with her intelligence, charm and sense of ceremonial which she had already displayed at the tender age of nine. In real life, she has been known to history as the Winter Queen or Elizabeth of Bohemia, from the short-lived reign there of her husband Frederick Prince of the Palatine. In the adversities which followed the rapid dispossession of the young couple, Elizabeth always displayed remarkable strength of character. She was also blessed with remarkable fertility, giving birth to a huge and vigorous family of thirteen children including the soldier prince Rupert of the Rhine and the princess Sophia whose descendants, the Hanoverians, still sit today on the British throne. While one cannot extrapolate the course of one marriage with a completely different man from another, there is reason to hope that the Anglo-French marriage of Elizabeth and a Bourbon prince would have resulted in a similar proliferation of heirs.

That is the optimistic prognosis to the success of the Gunpowder Plot. Alternatively one could argue more pessimistically that there is an inexorable beat to the march of history. With religious strife continuing in England between Catholics and High Church Anglicans, and Puritans, coupled with the (legitimate) dynastic claims to the English throne of the young Scottish king, Charles, one can easily envisage hostilities between the two countries escalating. There might have been a war in, say, 1639 (the date in real life of the First Anglo-Scottish so-called Bishops' war) . . . Perhaps after all fate is not so easily outwitted. Let us go further and imagine King Charles captured, tried, and the warrant for his execution signed by his unwilling – but in the end royally ruthless – sister, Queen Elizabeth II on 30 January 1649 . . .

And the rhyme the children would sing around the bonfire?

> Please to remember the fifth of November
> Gunpowder Freedom and Plot.
> We know no reason why Gunpowder Freedom
> Should ever be forgot.

Of course they ask for a penny for (King) Jamie, not the Guy.

King Charles I Wins the English Civil War

John Adamson

In the summer of 1643, Charles I, King of Great Britain and Ireland, had been engaged in putting down a major rebellion in his English kingdom for almost exactly a year. It was the most serious revolt against royal authority since the Northern Rising against Queen Elizabeth in 1569. The current revolt, however, was wholly different in scale. Charles spoke of it dismissively as 'the rebellion of the Earl of Essex' (the Parliamentarians' commander-in-chief), yet the rebels controlled Parliament, the city of London and large tracts of the English counties, particularly in the south-east. Furthermore, their sophisticated propaganda machine had persuaded many that the King was the dupe of a 'Popish plot' to subvert Protestantism within all three Stuart kingdoms.

By July 1643, however, the Parliamentarian rebellion looked set to go the way of its Elizabethan predecessor. Major garrison towns were falling to the Royalists. Most of the rebels' regional armies had been destroyed and the rebel political leadership, based at Westminster, was beginning to show signs of panic. To complete the King's good fortune, in early July came the news that his wife and consort, Henriette Marie, having spent much of the last six months raising money for the Royalist war effort, was about to return. For the uxorious King, public triumph and private happiness looked set to converge.

The moment provided an opportunity for royal theatricality that Charles, with his taste for masque and choreography, was not slow to exploit. The King had always treated his own marital felicity with his consort – a rarity among monarchs – as an ideal of the amity and concord that should prevail within the macrocosm of the realm. Hence, the July reunion of husband and wife, earlier forced apart by the exigencies of war, was recast as a metaphor for the reuniting of the kingdom – the larger 'coming together' of the divided nation that was possible now that the rebels were on the brink of defeat. In a brilliant *coup de théâtre*, Charles decided to stage his reunion with the Queen on the actual battlefield of Edgehill, in Warwickshire – the site where the one (and, it now seemed, only) large-scale battle of the war had taken place in October the previous year. Indeed, to emphasise his regained mastery of his kingdom, Charles deliberately scaled down his military escort to and from Edgehill to peacetime proportions: merely two troops of horse (or roughly 120 cavalrymen). Had there been a rebel force of any size in the vicinity, the King and Queen would have been defenceless. This, of course, was precisely Charles's point: Parliament no longer posed a serious military threat. And the taunting barb struck home; as one Roundhead news-writer commented bitterly, the 'King and Queene come from Edge-hill [to Oxford] . . . not being freighted out of their pace at all by the least Gun-shot of the Parliament's side'.

Once at Oxford (the wartime seat of the court), the imagery of domestic reunion was replaced by that of military triumph. On 14 July, the day after the Edgehill meeting, Charles and 'Queen Mary' staged a ceremonial entry into Oxford. Church bells pealed, salutes were fired, and an effusive speech by the University's Public Orator, Dr William Strode, accurately summed up the prevailing mood. 'You have left behind you Victory in the North,' he declaimed before the Queen; 'You find it spreading in the South; and Victory from the West hath been seasonably stayed till this poynt, as ordain'd to salute your approach and celebrate Your entertainment.'

'Seasonably stayed till this poynt' was Strode's archly donnish joke. For only the previous day, as Charles and Henriette Marie had been embracing on the now peaceful battlefield of Edgehill, his general, Sir Ralph Hopton, had been routing the rebel Parliament's major army in the west, under Sir William Waller, at Roundway Down, a mile north of Devizes. For all practical purposes, Parliament's military power in the west had been annihilated.

Waller's defeat crowned an extraordinary summer of Royalist conquest. Parliament's main army in the north-east – under Lord Fairfax and his son, Sir Thomas Fairfax – had been comprehensively defeated by the Earl of Newcastle. In the north-west, the Parliamentarians had been forced to abandon the siege of Chester for lack of troops, leaving the King with unobstructed use of a port that was ideally placed for landing military reinforcements from Ireland. In the south-west, Waller's defeat had given the King's forces almost uncontested control. And in East Anglia, the Earl of Newcastle had already advanced deep into Lincolnshire – Gainsborough capitulated on 30 July, and Stamford was shortly afterwards abandoned by its Parliamentarian garrison as indefensible – and seemed poised to threaten London from the north. As Oliver Cromwell, at the time a relatively obscure provincial cavalry commander, wrote on 6 August, 'there is nothing to interrupt an enemy [advancing south] but our horse'.

The position with the major ports – the strategically vital cities that controlled much of the country's trade, travel and communications – was scarcely better. Newcastle, which fed the coal supply to London, was also in the King's hands, and by mid-July it was obvious that the capital faced an impending fuel crisis, there being 'now a very great scarcity [of coal] in and about London'. Parliament-held Hull and Exeter were both besieged by the Royalists and likely to fall. Even London, the seat of the rebel administration, gave cause for concern. Resentment of wartime taxation had fuelled a new political movement for 'peace at any price' – in effect, voluntary capitulation to the King. To ease its growing unpopularity in the City, the Parliamentarian leadership in mid-July granted the capital complete exemption from all exactions for a period of two months – depriving itself of its richest source of revenue in the process.

As Parliament's military campaign faltered, the capital was swept with reports of conspiracies and plots. In London, plans were uncovered for a pro-Cavalier *coup d'état* organised by the Commons-man, Edmund Waller, and implicating some of the most senior Roundhead grandees. In Yorkshire, two of the county's most prominent Parliament-men, Sir John Hotham and his son, had only narrowly been prevented from betraying Hull to the Cavaliers – an act of treachery to Parliament (and loyalty to the King) for which they were subsequently executed.

The allegiance of Parliament's commander-in-chief, the Earl of Essex, also came under suspicion. When Essex wrote to Parliament on 9 July, offering two alternatives – a quasi-Arthurian trial by battle (which, with the current state of the armies, Parliament seemed certain to lose), or the immediate opening of negotiations with the King (which seemed certain to result in virtually surrender terms) – the letter was widely interpreted as a declaration that the commander-in-chief had given up the will to fight. The political struggle that ensued, to replace Essex with the younger and more dynamic (if hardly more successful) Sir William Waller, divided the Parliament throughout July, and effectively paralysed the Parliamentarian war effort. By the end of July, morale in Essex's haphazardly funded army – the Parliament-party's principal fighting force – was so low that troops were deserting even faster than new recruits could be sent up from London. Its total strength, both cavalry and infantry, had sunk to 2,500 men.

By the first week of August, London looked like a capital that was about to fall. There were 'such fears of the instant approaching of the Cavaliers', reported the London newsbook, *The Kingdomes Weekly Intelligencer*, on 8 August, 'that [many citizens] were about to ship their goods for Holland'. Parliament responded with an order forbidding any except merchant traders sending goods abroad, but this was not sufficient to halt the rumours that the leaders of the 'war party' in Parliament, Viscount Saye and Sele and John Pym, 'had conveyed beyond Sea many chests of money, to great value'.

The rumours against Saye and Pym were a libel. But by the end of July, many of those who had been in the forefront of Parliament's war effort in 1642 had decided to cut their losses and make their peace with the royal court, while there was still any political capital to made by doing so. During the first two weeks of August, six senior Roundhead peers – the Earls of Bedford, Holland, Clare, Portland, Viscount Conway, and Lord Lovelace – abandoned Parliament and threw themselves on the King's mercy at Oxford. Holland's defection, in particular, shocked and scandalised the party he left behind. Not only was he an experienced, if undistinguished, soldier (he had served as Lieutenant General of the Horse in the 1640 war against Scotland); he was also the first cousin and principal counsellor of Parliament's general, Essex. If Holland could defect to Oxford, might not Essex follow?

Even those within the Parliament-party's leadership who did not defect or desert immediately were quietly securing their escape routes in the event of Parliament's demise. The Earl of Northumberland – the greatest of all the aristocratic magnates on the Parliament's side – withdrew to his Sussex country seat, Petworth, in mid-August, in readiness to join the exodus to Oxford. He had been making preparations for the contingency for at least a fortnight. On 1 August he had arranged for £2,000 (the equivalent of an entire year's income for an affluent landed gentleman) to be made available immediately in cash, borrowing the money from Adrian May, one of the principal financiers involved with the Oxford court – and the banker who had earlier arranged the pawning of the English crown jewels to finance Charles's war. Northumberland had had enough; the grandest of all the rebels was about to make his peace with the King.

The catalyst for this exodus was yet another Royalist

victory, one that seemed finally to place Parliament's defeat beyond doubt. Four days earlier, on the morning of 27 July, Bristol, the kingdom's most important port after London, had surrendered to the King after putting up only brief resistance to the Royalist assault. Well fortified, well supplied, and provided with a large garrison, Bristol had seemed impregnable to attack. News of its surrender therefore inevitably prompted allegations of foul play on the part of its governor, Colonel Nathaniel Fiennes, who was arrested, pending trial by court martial. 'The direful news of the surrender of Bristol', wrote the Royalist Sir Edward Hyde, 'struck them to the heart, and came upon them [the Parliamentarians] as a sentence of death.'

Now, only London and the south-east – the original heartlands of the rebellion – remained securely in Parliamentarian control and, even here, it was evident that support for the revolt was waning fast. During July there had been a pro-Royalist insurrection in Kent which had exposed the extent of disaffection against Parliamentarian rule. With more than two-thirds of the kingdom and almost all the major ports under Royalist control, the way was now clear for Charles to concentrate his forces for an assault on London, the nerve-centre of the rebellion. At last, Charles could make 'an end of the war'. The opportunity was clearly in the sights of the victorious Royalist generals at Bristol. A council of war, convened by the King on 3 August, seems to have been in general agreement as to the ultimate objective, the fall of London. But there were two rival views as to how this would be most effectively achieved. One was an immediate advance on the capital, a lightning attack which would capitalise on the Parliamentarians' current disarray. The alternative proposal, put by Sir John Culpeper, temporarily postponed the advance on London until the rebel garrison at Gloucester – the one significant pocket of resistance remaining between Bristol and Lancashire – had been subdued.

After prolonged argument, the Gloucester-then-London

strategy prevailed. What seems to have carried the debate was not a belief that the Gloucester route was militarily more prudent; rather, a confidence – under the prevailing circumstances far from irrational – that the Parliament's military position was now so weak as to be irrecoverable. The extra few days required for the detour to Gloucester (where the immediate surrender of its governor, Colonel Edward Massie, had been promised) would help encourage London to accept the pointlessness of further resistance. Indeed, Royalist writers were already preparing discourses for the press, in anticipation of London's fall. The Royalist polemicist, James Howell, in a work that was partly printed and then abandoned when overtaken by events, looked forward to the capital's day of reckoning: 'for the anger of a King is like the roaring of a Lyon, and I never read yet of any City that contested with her Soveraigne, but she smarted soundly for it at last'. By August at the latest, it seemed, Charles would be back in Whitehall, and able to ponder at leisure how best to make London 'smart'.

Yet London did not fall. Nor did Gloucester, the King's immediate objective. Instead, by the end of August, Charles's apparently inexorable juggernaut had been halted, never to recover the momentum it had attained in those victorious weeks that had culminated in the fall of Bristol. What had gone wrong?

To many of Charles's contemporaries, the decision to divert his army to Gloucester, rather than to advance on London, was the error that cost him the war. Sir Richard Bulstrode, the adjutant to Lord Wilmot and an officer who served during the Gloucester campaign, was emphatic that in August London's capture was an achievable goal. 'If the King had then marched to London, he had, in al Probability, made an End of the War. But he was ill (if not maliciously) perswaded to besiege Gloucester, which was the only Place left to the Parliament in these [western] Parts . . . Thus, when the King's Affairs were in a prosperous Condition, he trifled away Time to no purpose in that unfortunate Siege.' Others concurred. The 'war party' within the Privy Council was enthusiastic for an immediate attack on the capital. And Henriette Marie, whose strategic judgements were often shrewder and always more decisive than her husband's, was another advocate of an immediate attack on London.

There are strong grounds for thinking that they were right. August was the month when the condition of the roads was usually at its best, and travel fastest. Had the King's army left Bristol at the beginning of the month, as Bulstrode and others had hoped, it could have reached the outskirts of London by around 14 or 15 August – fully a week before the faction-riven Parliament was able to put together its army for the relief of Gloucester. During the first weeks of August, Parliament's ability to defend itself plumbed the lowest point it was ever to reach in the course of the Civil War. With Essex's army reduced to a demoralised rump of barely 2,500, Waller's all but destroyed, and the only alternative an improvised force of untried citizen volunteers – which had yet to be mustered, let alone turned into a coherent fighting force – the capital was highly vulnerable. Its ancient walls were useless against modern artillery, and the makeshift ring of forts and earthwork defences that had been strung out around the suburbs – the so-called 'Lines of Communication' – were so extensive and so hastily constructed as to be almost indefensible.

No doubt, the City's Puritan Lord Mayor, John Venn, would have tried to rally the citizenry. Yet there would probably have been no battle for London. A Royalist advance on the city would have accelerated the haemorrhaging of support that had been sapping the Parliament's authority steadily since mid-July. There would have been more Bedfords and Hollands going over to the King's party, more officers in key positions for London's defence – like Sir John Conyers, the Lieutenant of the Tower – requesting leave for an extended period of foreign travel. Had the defections among the nobility continued, as was likely, it is hard to believe that Essex himself (who, two years later, was working intensively for the King's restoration on the most lenient of terms) would have been far behind. The City's merchant community would have been unlikely to risk the plundering that was the soldier's entitlement if the capital were taken by force. No sooner would Charles's army have appeared on Hounslow Heath than pressure on the City authorities – and on whatever was left of Parliament – for surrender would have become irresistible.

How, then, did Charles pass up what contemporaries believed to have been an almost failsafe route to victory? The critical problem was the opportunities that were opened up to his opponents by the Royalists' delay. It was not until 10 August that Charles and his army appeared before the walls of Gloucester; and by that time the city's strongly Puritan government had overruled Massie and resolved to carry on the fight. From that moment, a point of honour dictated that Charles commit his army to a siege, even if he had wished to press ahead with his assault against London. The army that had successfully stormed Bristol was kept immobilised outside the walls of Gloucester for four weeks.

In the interim, the Parliamentarians acquired the time to resolve enough of their internal differences to reaffirm Essex as commander-in-chief and to create a new army, some 8,000 strong and almost entirely composed of London's citizen soldiers – members of the London trained bands – with the sole objective of raising the siege of Gloucester and forestalling the King's advance. At Gloucester, Massie held out; and on 5 September Charles abandoned the siege, rather than face a set-piece battle with Essex's newly arrived expeditionary force. The tactical plan he had devised after the fall of Bristol, against the better judgement of many of his officers, had gone disastrously awry. The opportunities opened up by his July victories had been squandered. They were never to recur.

Yet there was almost a month – roughly from mid-July until mid-August that year – when, in Sir Richard Bulstrode's phrase, the King might, 'in al Probability, [have] made an End of the War'. That probability was no mere idle fancy. For many at Westminster, it had a compelling force that dictated their immediate political calculations. It prompted the many shifts and tergiversations – the arrangements for money to be sent abroad, the sudden resignations from military commands, the timely desertions of Parliament's apparently sinking ship – that characterised Westminster politics in the high summer of 1643. What sort of England did contemporaries think would emerge in the aftermath of this expected Royalist victory?

There was no shortage of predictions. War is inevitably premised on a series of contemporary exercises in 'virtual history'. For each belligerent party only takes up arms because, if defeated, it expects a malign future that it is the purpose of victory to render counterfactual. As delineated in their public propaganda, the Parliamentarians' expectations had three key elements. Should the Cavaliers prevail – so it was claimed – the liberties of the subject would be subverted, Parliaments would be destroyed, and the English Church would fall victim to creeping popery – a court-based conspiracy to subvert the Protestant settlement and move the usage of the parishes ever closer to the doctrine and liturgical practice of the 'Whore of Rome'. To what extent would these predictions have been realised in the post-rebellion government of Charles I?

In August, to the sound of pealing church bells and the acclamations of the crowd, Charles would have made his triumphal entry into his vanquished capital. A *Te Deum* would have been sung in the Chapel Royal and every hack poet in London would have published his contribution to the mountain of sycophantic doggerel that invariably marked any major princely jubilee. The structures of government would have been familiar. The centre of power in 1643

Restoration England would, once again, have been the royal court. Whitehall Palace had been locked up and unused during the almost two years of the court's absence, but apart from the 'raw scent' of damp it was ready for the King's immediate accommodation. In the autumn, the point in the year when the court usually reconvened in Westminster, the tapestries would have been rehung, the Turkey carpets unrolled, the heavy, velvet-upholstered furniture taken out of storage, and the outward splendour of court life would have been resumed as it had been before the King's hasty departure back in January 1642.

Yet, the grandiloquent rhetoric of courtly display belied a more complex series of political realities that would have tempered the exercise of postwar monarchical power. Much as Charles may have wished it otherwise, the character of the restored regime would inevitably have been affected by the terms on which he had induced his constituency to fight for him in 1642. The 'King's party' had expectations of him that, at least initially, he could not afford to disregard.

Perhaps the central Royalist expectation was that the King they had fought for in 1642 was bound by law. In this regard, one of Charles's greatest successes in the year leading up to the outbreak of war in the summer of 1642 – indeed, one of the reasons why he had been able to create a 'King's party' to resist the Parliament's opposition – had been his reinvention of himself (and the institution of monarchy) as the guardian of the law. Many of those who had joined the King's war effort in 1642 did so because they believed that Parliament was acting outside the law. An unrepresentative Puritan clique or 'junto' had captured control of Parliament and was manipulating it – in part, through the intimidation that it could bring to bear through the London mob – in order to advance a programme of change to the life of the Church that was as controversial and innovatory as anything that had been attempted in the 1630s by Charles and his supposedly 'Popishly affected' bishops. From 1641, the Puritan junto in

Parliament threatened to ban the use of the Book of Common Prayer, permitted the smashing of altars and images in churches, and looked set to allow the character of the Church to be determined by a series of mostly elderly, Puritan zealots. Against these new, Parliament-sponsored 'innovations', Charles was able to present himself as a bulwark of ecclesiastical moderation, the defender of the Church as it had existed 'in King James's time', and the guardian of the law.

Charles's new image as a monarch who intended to rule within the law was based on practical foundations. Between the 'despotic' excesses of the 1630s and the resort to arms in 1642 there lay an entire year of major political reforms – the constitutional 'revolution' of 1641 – during which the King had conceded extensive limitations on his personal and prerogative powers. By the end of 1641, he had already accepted that Parliaments would henceforth meet every three years; the current Parliament could not be dissolved without its own consent; the 'arbitrary' prerogative and ecclesiastical courts (notably Star Chamber and High Commission) should be abolished; the series of prerogative-based schemes for raising revenue independently from Parliament – from 'Ship Money' to forest fines – were illegal; and that no taxation could be imposed without the subject's consent, as signified in Parliament.

The success with which the King had reinvented himself as a 'parliamentary prince' during 1641 inevitably determined the tone and polemical thrust of Royalist apologetic during the war. Its consistency is striking. Unsurprisingly, the 'King's party' did not represent itself as a band of would-be 'absolutists' intent on creating an authoritarian state, unanswerable to any elected assembly. Instead, from Charles's famous *Answer to the Nineteen Propositions* (his reply to Parliament's ultimatum of June 1642), there was a repeated emphasis on the Parliament-respecting, law-abiding nature of the Caroline regime: Charles, the would-be autocrat of the 1630s, had been recast as a reformed and, in some respects,

51

penitent monarch. This is why the claim to be fighting 'for King and Parliament' was as much a Royalist as a Parliamentarian slogan in 1642 – and why, with relatively few exceptions, it was a claim that carried conviction.

If Charles, after a 1643 victory, would have been the prisoner of his own rhetoric, he would also, more practically, have been the prisoner of the impecuniousness of the Crown. Around the year 1600, the Crown had been able to fund almost forty per cent of the monarch's 'ordinary' expenditure (the costs of running court and government, excluding war) from his landed estate, with the majority of the remaining sixty per cent coming from the customs revenues. Yet forty years later, after massive land-sales by the Crown in the first decades of the century, these proportions had fundamentally changed. By 1640, only fourteen per cent of royal expenditure was able to be funded from the Crown's landed estate, with a massive eighty-six per cent of expenditure being funded from non-parliamentary prerogative sources (in particular the customs) – almost all of which were to be declared illegal by Parliament in the course of 1641.

It was to these harsh financial realities that a victorious Charles I would have returned in 1643. Parliament's capture of the customs revenues in 1641 (when the legislature had still contained many future Cavaliers) meant that no king, in future, could govern without first devising a workable financial *modus vivendi* with his legislature. Assuming that the restored Charles I were to live no more extravagantly than he had until 1640, he would still have had to rely on Parliament to make up almost *nine-tenths* of his ordinary revenues. And besides the ordinary expenditure of government, there were still heavy military commitments ahead, requiring what contemporaries called 'extraordinary revenues' – or yet more Parliament-approved taxation.

Chief among those military commitments was the need to suppress the Catholic rebellion in Ireland (which had broken out in October 1641). While no one seriously doubted that the Irish rebellion could be suppressed, given adequate funding, a new English expeditionary force would have had to be raised, and this, too, would have tied the King still more closely to Parliament (and, no doubt, to its members' demands for the large-scale expropriation of Irish lands). Indeed, the Catholic Irish stood to lose almost as much from a Royalist victory in 1643 as from a Parliamentarian one. While the Cromwellian massacres might well have been avoided, that the King's postwar freedom of action would be fettered by the expectations of a future Cavalier Parliament was clearly foreseen by the Irish Catholics' provisional government, the Confederation of Kilkenny. In the summer of 1643, when a victory for the King's party in England was clearly in sight, a group of senior Confederates offered the papal envoy, the Oratorian Father, Pierfrancesco Scarampi, their assessment of what was likely to happen: 'the king, should he succeed by the aid of the [English] Protestants, would be, in a manner, engaged to them. They, as usual, would oppose freedom of religion [to Catholics] in Ireland, and insist on the punishment of our "rebellion", as they style it, to enable them to seize our properties and occupy our estates.'

Nor was Ireland the only context in which military involvement was likely to heighten the Crown's dependency on Lords and Commons. One of the central political issues of the late 1630s had been whether Charles should intervene militarily to assist his Wittelsbach nephew, the Prince-Elector (*Kurfürst*) of the Palatinate (and brother of Princes Rupert and Maurice), whose father had been dispossessed of his lands by the Catholic Habsburgs in the 1620s, at the beginning of the Thirty Years War. With the reconsolidation of Charles's rule in England, that issue was certain to re-emerge. Prince Rupert looked set to become the leader of a new 'Palatine group' at Charles's court. Having played so prominent a part in restoring his uncle to his English possessions, he could hardly be denied his uncle's help in recovering his family's possessions in the Rhine Palatinate. Nor was there a more propitious time to do so. A French army under the Prince de Condé had just smashed the Imperial forces at Rocroi. Habsburg power appeared to be on the wane; in the Palatinate, as in Ireland, Charles looked likely to be on the winning side.

England may have been pacified, and Ireland conquered. Yet would Scotland, the kingdom that had initiated the revolt against Charles's Personal Rule, have sat idly by and seen its 'godly brethren', the English Parliamentarians, vanquished by Charles's godless Cavaliers? By August 1643, talk of the Scots sending an army to aid the beleaguered Roundheads had been current for months. Later in 1643, it was to culminate in an Anglo-Scottish treaty, under the terms of which Scotland was to send an army of some 21,000 men into England to intervene on the Parliamentarian side. Whatever victories Charles won in England in the summer of 1643, surely all would have been undone with the arrival of this formidable force of anti-Royalist Scots?

Yet there are strong reasons for believing that, if Charles had taken London in August 1643, Scottish military assistance to the Parliamentarians would never have been forthcoming. As late as that August, the English Parliament had still not concluded any defensive alliance with the Scottish Covenanters, and if Charles had brought the English revolt to a close in early August there seems little doubt that the negotiations in Edinburgh between the English Parliamentarian delegation and the Scots would have collapsed.

Nor were the Scots unanimous that aid to the Parliament should be forthcoming. In August 1643, far from being at war with Scotland, Charles was scrupulously maintaining his diplomatic relations with the government in Edinburgh. Much as he might have disapproved of Presbyterian ('Covenanter') rule in Scotland, which had been forced on him as a result of the Scots' victory at Newburn in August 1640, the Edinburgh regime still contained a strong 'King's party', centred on the Marquess of Hamilton; and this would have been immeasurably strengthened in the event of a Royalist victory in England. In Scotland, the proposal to force reform of the English Church by backing one side in England's Civil War was already controversial. Had the Covenanters' prospective allies been defeated, the idea of the Scots invading England to topple a victorious Charles I would have been highly improbable – so long as Charles continued to abide by the terms of the 1641 Anglo-Scottish treaties, as, hitherto, he had shown every intention of doing. As late as August 1643, when the King was clearly winning in England, he rejected an offer from the Earl of Montrose to raise an anti-Covenanter army on his behalf in Scotland; the Marquess of Hamilton, on the other hand, who had taken the Scottish Covenant and counselled him against Montrose, he raised to a dukedom. Forestalling an alliance between the English Parliament and the Scottish Covenanters would not have been the only diplomatic benefit to flow from a Royalist victory in August 1643. It would also have saved the King from the most politically damaging of all his wartime escapades: the deal, concluded on 15 September with the Con-federates in Ireland, whereby he agreed to suspend hostilities in order to recruit Catholic Irish troops for service in Eng-land against the Parliamentarians. More than any other of Charles's actions, his approval of this Irish 'Cessation' seemed to confirm Parliamentarian claims that he was in league with popery. In August, however, the Cessation treaty was still in negotiation. Had victory come in England in mid-August, it would never have been signed. Without it, advocates of this Royalist–Irish Catholic coalition would have lost much of their influence within the Privy Council, and Charles would have been spared his greatest public-relations disaster of the 1640s.

The postwar English Church also looked set to assume a very different trajectory to that which it had taken during the ascendancy of Charles's controversial Archbishop of Canterbury, William Laud. Here, too, the King would have been constrained not only by the public commitments he had made between 1641 and 1643, but also by the men he had chosen to promote during that period as guarantees of his own solidly Protestant credentials. By 1643, it was clear that Charles had turned his back on Laud. The aged prelate, impeached by Parliament and incarcerated in the Tower, had become *persona non grata* in Royalist circles, an embarrassing relic of a programme of ceremonialist Church reforms that had clearly failed. One question remained, however: had the King also turned his back on 'Laudianism' – the series of ceremonial and doctrinal innovations that Laud had promoted in the 1630s Church; in particular, an emphasis on sacramentalism over preaching, an overt hostility to the Church's Elizabethan and Jacobean Calvinist inheritance, and a campaign to restore both churches and churchmen to their pre-Reformation affluence and prestige?

This was one question that Charles had already anticipated. On the eve of his expected victory, in the last week of July 1643, the King staged an extraordinary public (and widely reported) oath-taking in Oxford in order to reassure doubters on this score. In the presence of the Primate of Ireland, Archbishop Ussher of Armagh, Charles swore on the sacrament: 'I do intend the establishment of the true Protestant Religion as it stood in its beauty, in the happy dayes of Queen Elizabeth without any connivance of Popery.' Likewise, the churchmen whom the King had promoted to serve at court between 1641 and 1643 had been selected with equal care to suggest that Charles's ecclesiastical tastes were now 'without any connivance of Popery'.

Of course, it is open to doubt how much of this trend reflects a real 'conversion of heart' on the King's part, and how much an adventitious outward show. Yet, whether or not Charles remained internally committed to the Laudian project (as is possible), the July oath-taking and the solemn vow to restore the Church to its Elizabethan purity reveals an uncharacteristically acute understanding of his own constituency's sensitivities. Even among most Royalists, aspects of the 1630s Laudian innovations had proved profoundly unpopular; and – in the short term, at least – Charles could not afford to offend the Cavaliers.

Paradoxically, then, a Restoration in the summer of 1643 is likely to have moved the *ecclesia Anglicana* in a far more 'Lower-Church' direction than happened after the Restoration of 1660. For in 1660 it was the exiled Laudians, the younger generation of Caroline divines, who returned to dominate the English Church. In 1643, it would have been the older Jacobean Calvinists, with Archbishops Ussher and John Williams of York as the chief court prelates, who would have set the tone – and an austerely anti-ceremonialist tone at that – for the development of the English Church. The future rebuilding of St Paul's Cathedral (to designs by Christopher Wren, the nephew of the ultra-Laudian bishop, Matthew Wren) as an English version of St Peter's Basilica in Rome, complete with a 'popish' dome, would have been unthinkable.

A Royalist victory in the summer of 1643 would not have brought a return to Clarendon's prewar 'halcyon days', an idyllic England of peace and plenty. Englishmen may have stopped killing each other, but that would not have been the end of the fighting. Charles's need to regain his Irish throne and the desirability of regaining his Scottish one would have entailed war for much of the rest of the decade. And so long as that was so, King and legislature would be locked, once again, in an uncomfortable but unavoidable embrace. No doubt there would have been another generation of Army Plotters – the contrivers of a series of failed military *coups d'état* against the Parliament in 1641 – who would be ready to try the same desperate (and wholly counter-productive) remedies once more. Yet, so long as the King needed money, a military coup against Parliament would have solved little. The English nobility and gentry had become far too adept at avoiding exactions they did not wish to pay.

For all the new equestrian statues commemorating Charles's brilliance as a general, and the mass-produced engravings of *Carolus Triumphator*, the victor of the English Civil War is likely to have proved a disappointed monarch. Despite the laurels of victory, Charles's plans to rebuild Whitehall Palace as a gigantic Escorial on the Thames looked certain to go unfulfilled – victims of a cash-strapped Exchequer. The seat of the 'King of Great Britain', as Charles liked to style himself, would continue to be the sprawling Tudor warren of Whitehall, what the Duc de Saint-Simon would later describe as 'the largest and ugliest palace in Europe'. The possibilities for creating an authoritarian, French-style monarchy, unconstrained by the unwelcome intrusion of any legislature – a prospect that had arguably been open to Charles at the end of the 1630s, had he been able to avoid a war – had closed for good after he had been forced to allow Parliament to reconvene in November 1640.

Even in victory, then, there was no going back. Henceforth, as Charles's son was to discover, the legislature's ability to control the power of the purse (which would have been even stronger in 1643 than it was to be in 1660) would act as a major constraint on the Crown's capacity for autonomous action. The mischievous genie that the 'Long Parliament' had allowed to escape in the tumultuous year 1641 was too much for even a victorious Charles I to rebottle.

Benedict Arnold Wins the Revolutionary War for Britain

Robert Cowley

The American Revolution was a war that Great Britain should have won. Only bad luck, some regrettable decisions, and the unpredictable intervention of the unexpected prevented the redcoats from decisively striking down the rebellion of the thirteen colonies. Many of the same standards of failure applied to the American rebel cause too. One can argue that the British were stretched too thin, that they lacked the manpower to bring a swift end to the colonial revolt. American distances undid them; so did American persistence and passion. The British might have won most of the battles; the Americans, only those that counted. In the end, the victorious difference may have been nothing more than home-field advantage. It was a long war – seven years of actual combat – and no wonder that counterfactual possibilities abound. A man of great faith like George Washington often saw the hand of Providence at work and, indeed, the unexpected seemed at times the only real certainty. The United States should by all rights have expired at birth. Today's most powerful nation on earth was hardly inevitable.

At home, the ever-patient Washington was the principal character in this drama, as was Benjamin Franklin in Europe. What if Franklin had failed to dazzle the French with his homespun shrewdness? Yet I have chosen to focus on another individual, one who several times could have made all the difference for both sides. He is the man who was, for the first three years of the Revolution, Washington's best fighting general, but who became, in the historian Carl Van Doren's words, 'the Iago of traitors', America's Antichrist, its fallen angel: Benedict Arnold.

Arnold had what one French observer called, in the eccentric spelling of the era, a *rage militair*. Courage was a gift. So was proclivity to offend, to eschew compromise; he lacked political good sense, and it would be his undoing. There was an undeniable magnetism about the man, and he inspired the devotion of those who served under him. Yet many recoiled from his combative arrogance, his open impatience with mediocre performance. He had pale eyes that could pierce and cajole at one moment and frost over the next. His long brow and prominent nose seemed to complement his powerful body. Arnold was an athlete who could perform gymnastic prodigies, the sort of alpha male who would not be denied. The physical qualities that obviously attracted his first wife were matched by his coldness; she came to loathe him. He had the addiction to ostentation of many self-made men. At the same time, he would not hesitate to endure the unforgiving rigours of the American wilderness, and persuaded men to endure them with him.

'Arnold's character – which thousands thought they knew so well when they heard him called a hero, and again when they heard him called a viper – remains hard to grasp,' the historian Charles Royster has written, in trying to define the mystery of the man. 'He sought extremes: The highest rank, the hardest march, the hottest combat, the most luxurious social display, the coolest secret calculation, the most decisive act of the war, the highest possible price. Whatever satisfaction those extremes seemed to promise always eluded him.'

Describing Becky Sharpe in *Vanity Fair*, Thackeray writes of 'the dismal precocity of poverty'. There was the same element in Arnold's make-up. He was the son of an alcoholic bankrupt, and the humiliations of his youth were built into his character. He was apprenticed as an apothecary and later set up his own shop in New Haven, Connecticut. While still in his twenties he branched out, becoming a merchant-trader and the owner of several vessels which ranged along the North American coast from Quebec to the West Indies. To avoid the frequently onerous trade duties that Great Britain imposed on her colonies, Arnold was not above smuggling. He prospered. By the time the Massachusetts Minute Men fired on the redcoats at Lexington and Concord in April 1775, he was deeply involved in the politics of revolution. He organised a militia company and marched off with it to George Washington's headquarters in Cambridge, where the Virginian was directing the siege of Boston. For all his veneer of self-confidence, the thirty-four-year-old Captain Arnold could hardly have foreseen the effect he would have on outcomes of the Revolution, both actual and possible.

Everybody gives Ethan Allen the credit for taking Fort Ticonderoga in 1775; few, however, remember (or probably care to) that Benedict Arnold was at his side when Allen carried out his feat of bloodless bluster. If Allen received the subsequent publicity, Arnold got what he wanted: Ticonderoga's artillery. Without it, Washington might never have taken Boston and the American Revolution might have stalled before it was one year old.

Ticonderoga stood on a bluff overlooking the southern end of Lake Champlain; in 1755 the French had built the star-shaped fortress to block a potential British advance into Canada. Three years later the British suffered hundreds of casualties in an unsuccessful storming of the fort. Now, as the Revolution began, though Ticonderoga remained a strategic prize, it was mainly used as a supply and weapons depot and held by a force of fewer than a hundred men. Its commander, a Captain William Delaplace, had been warned that the Americans, notably Allen and the frontier ruffians he called the Green Mountain Boys, might try something. Delaplace did not take the threat seriously. Yet he should have done so. The territory we now know as Vermont was then called the New Hampshire Grants; it was claimed by both New

Hampshire and New York. Allen, who dreamed of a separate colony between the two, led guerrilla attacks on New York settlements in the Grants. He saw the taking of Ticonderoga as a coup (and also as an opportunity for plunder, including the fort's substantial supply of rum).

Meanwhile in Cambridge, Arnold persuaded the Massachusetts Committee of Safety to let him attempt to seize Ticonderoga, and especially its guns. The Continentals might have had plenty of willing musketmen, but they had few cannon. Haste was important; could he reach Ticonderoga before the British reinforced it? As it turned out, he needn't have worried. Arnold, by now a colonel, linked up with Allen, who was hardly pleased to see the new arrival. Arnold may have had the one official commission to lead, but this was Allen's turf. In the end, they decided to share command.

They counted on surprise and the cover of darkness and a gusty rainstorm. At 4 a.m. on 10 May, the Americans burst through the main wicket gate; the single sentry aimed his musket at Allen but it failed to fire. He ran. While the Green Mountain Boys swarmed over the fort, routing out sleeping soldiers and looking for alcohol, Arnold and Allen galloped up a flight of stairs to the quarters of the commander. Delaplace, breeches in hand, stumbled to the door. He asked by whose authority he should hand over the fort? Allen, according to his own later account, uttered the now-famous words: 'In the name of the great Jehovah, and the Continental Congress.' (An ear-witness had a somewhat different, and less eloquent, version, something to the effect of: 'Come out of there, you damned old bastard.')

The fort had fallen in less than ten minutes. Allen's men found their plunder; Arnold, his cannon. But it was not until the winter that Washington dispatched his Colonel Commandant of Artillery, the huge Henry Knox, to bring the guns back. Floating some fifty of them down the lake on boats and scows, and then transferring them to oxen-drawn sledges, Knox brought the guns 300 miles across the Berkshires and the snowy hills of Massachusetts. On the night of 4 March 1776, Washington's Continentals put the cannon in place on Dorchester Heights, overlooking Boston. He had trumped the British, who were forced to evacuate the city soon after.

Consider what might have happened if those cannon had not turned up on Dorchester Heights. The British positions around Boston were all but impregnable. A contemplated American attempt to storm them would have been not just costly but possibly disastrous. Had there been no Ticonderoga guns, the redcoats could have thrust at the Americans with ease – which they also planned to do – driving them away from Boston. The result in either case might not have been the immediate end of the rebellion, but something that would ultimately have doomed it: the discrediting and removal of George Washington.

Arnold's first martial success soon turned sour; it became a pattern. Allen hogged the credit. His drunken Green Mountain Boys stripped Arnold of command at gunpoint. Arnold asked the Massachusetts provincial legislature for repayment of money he had advanced, but the legislature baulked. He then learned that his wife had died.

In the midsummer of 1775 Arnold returned to Cambridge, full of a bold new scheme. He got George Washington's ear. The American commander was impressed by Arnold's raspy-voiced enthusiasm and his proposal to attack the fortress city of Quebec. Reports indicated that Quebec was held by no more than a few hundred men. He would hit from an unexpected flank, the wilderness of Maine. Meanwhile, another American force would work northward along the Lake Champlain corridor, taking Montreal and then linking with Arnold at Quebec. Arnold's plan was as bold as it was risky; this was a heady time when anything seemed possible. The Americans were yet to discover their limitations.

Arnold's overland march is one of the genuine epics of American history; people of the time compared it to

Hannibal's crossing of the Alps, minus the elephants. From the beginning there were delays, small ones at first, but they began to add up. Fall had come by the time that Arnold and the thousand-odd men he led reached the mouth of the Kennebec River in Maine. There he found 200 heavy, flat-bottomed bateaux waiting for him, but they had been quickly put together from green lumber that was bound to shrink and crack. Days were lost while he waited for them to be caulked and replacements built. Meanwhile, scouts brought back information that was encouraging, but inaccurate. The maps Arnold relied on proved worthless. He estimated that his route was 180 miles long, but it was more like 350. Instead of a predicted twenty days, he needed forty.

The use of bateaux was a mistake; lighter, faster canoes would have been much more appropriate for river travel. Four men were needed to carry an emptied bateau around waterfalls or across portage paths barely wide enough to accommodate a single man; later, they had to be shouldered over granite heights. They shattered on rocky rapids or tipped over. Water spoiled much of the food supply. Men began to suffer from fevers and diarrhoea. There were swamps that from afar looked like meadows – until one reached them and sank to one's waist in freezing slime. Promising watercourses led nowhere and had to be retraced, costing more time. On 21 October, a late-season hurricane swept over the expedition; the river rose twelve feet and was too swollen to negotiate. More food and gear was lost. Men were reduced to eating candles and trying to make soup from deerskin moccasins. At 'Camp Disaster', Arnold and his officers held a council of war. They voted to go on – all except one colonel, who was still downriver. He turned back, and took 350 men and all the expedition's medical supplies with him.

Arnold recognised that he now had too few men, at 650, to take Quebec by storm, unless the British were not yet 'apprised of our coming'. But they were. Messages to French-Canadian sympathisers had been intercepted. Too late Arnold abandoned his bateaux. Now in Canada, he reached outlying settlements. He paid friendly French-Canadians for cattle and sent back beef on the hoof; his starving men thought they were dreaming. On 9 November the modern Hannibal reached Point Lévis on the St Lawrence River, just two-thirds of a mile across from Quebec. Arnold could see two British men-of-war riding at anchor. They had arrived just days earlier, bringing several hundred redcoat reinforcements. The British, tipped off to his approach, had also destroyed all watercraft on the southern shore of the river, forcing Arnold to scour the area for canoes. The odds against him were lengthening.

Yet Arnold did get across and camped on the Plains of Abraham, where James Wolfe had won his famous victory in 1759. He tried to negotiate, hoping to bluff the garrison into surrender, but was rebuffed. His best hope now was to wait for Brigadier General Richard Montgomery, the former British officer who had just taken Montreal. Montgomery did not show up until the beginning of December, bringing only 300 men with him. The two commanders recognised that a conventional siege was impossible. They could not dig parallel trenches in the frozen ground, and they had only a few pitiful artillery pieces. Even so, they decided to go ahead with an attack. On 31 December, under cover of a snowstorm, they hit the city from two sides. Their hope was to force the lower walls, meet, and fight their way up, house by house if necessary, into the main town. Grapeshot killed Montgomery; a bullet smashed Arnold's left leg. The attack petered out, but even so the Americans maintained their siege. For six months, until 10,000 British reinforcements arrived, all of the province of Quebec, except for the couple of square miles within the walls of the city, was part of America.

Arnold later maintained that if he had arrived ten days sooner, Quebec would have been his. For Americans, it may be tempting to think of the province as the fourteenth state – until they consider the headache that a Catholic Quebec would have proved to an otherwise Protestant nation. What kind of difficulties might Canadian representatives have presented at the Constitutional Convention of 1787? The divisive issues of slavery and the stand-off of large and small states were problems enough. Would Quebec have in turn seceded from the former secessionist colonies? Might we have eventually had, instead of a Louisiana Purchase from France, a Louisiana Swap?

The British thousands who arrived in May 1776 might have besieged the American-held city and eventually won it back, along with the rest of the province as well. As it was, they chased the Americans out of Canada. Yet what if they had moved with a greater sense of urgency? They might have brought the American Revolution to a premature conclusion, for, apart from Washington's Boston victory, the year 1776 – the year of the Declaration of Independence – witnessed one Patriot débâcle after another. It was apparent after the rout of the Americans in Quebec that the British, whose Canadian army would grow to 13,000 by the end of the summer, were getting ready for a southward drive along the Lake Champlain corridor.

The retaking of Fort Ticonderoga would be Britain's first order of military business, followed by a march on Albany, a town that they saw as a magnet for Loyalist resistance. That spring, meanwhile, Washington had led his forces to New York City. He anticipated a British invasion but he was taking a risk. If the enemy defeated the Americans there, the entire Hudson River would be open; converging British armies could seal off New England, with its abundance of supplies and manpower, from the rest of the rebellious colonies. At the end of August, at the Battle of Long Island, Sir William Howe's redcoats battered, and nearly trapped, Washington and his army. Only the cover of a sudden fog allowed the Americans to escape across the East River to Manhattan. Small wonder Washington saw the hand of Providence at work. Nonetheless, the Americans continued to reel from defeat to defeat. That fall it increasingly began to look as though the British were a campaign or two away from putting the American Revolution down for good. Yet once again, Benedict Arnold would save the Patriot cause, this time in the improbable role of naval commander.

That summer, Major General Horatio Gates, another former British officer who now commanded the remnants of the American Canadian force, made Arnold, lately promoted to brigadier general, commodore of the tiny Lake Champlain flotilla. Arnold was the only American land commander who had actually been a sailor. He learned that the British were assembling ships, and large ones, at the head of the lake. It should take them no more than two months to mass for a combined amphibious operation; he estimated early September at the latest. His best, indeed his only, hope was to delay the British long enough to compel them to suspend their advance until the following year. On 1 September Arnold headed up the lake to make a reconnaissance in force. When Guy Carleton, the British Governor of Canada who was in charge of the expedition, learned of Arnold's approach, indecision gripped him. Was his fleet large enough to beat Arnold's? He elected to hold off his advance until work on a 180-ton sloop-of-war was completed. Almost a month passed before the ship was in the water, yet though the season was late the British still held the advantage.

Carleton's delay was an unexpected benefit, and it gave Arnold time to scout out a place to make a stand. He knew that he had no chance in the open lake. But he came on a spruce-covered hummock called Valcour Island that was separated from the New York shore by half a mile of water, a narrow channel like the one Themistocles defended against the Persians at Salamis. This would help to equalise the forces. He placed his sixteen ill-assorted craft in a crescent-shaped formation; they were turned broadside to the south, the direction from which the British would probably come. The leaves were turning, and snow appeared on the mountains that flanked the lake. Arnold waited.

It wasn't until 11 October that the British finally appeared, proceeding downlake on a strong northerly breeze. Carleton's force had twice the number of fighting craft, twice the armament of Arnold's little flotilla. But the narrow channel and the fact that the British would be obliged to head into the wind reduced their advantages. Not only would they have to enter the bay one by one, but they would also have a difficult time forming and holding a battle line.

Arnold's plan worked; only one British schooner actually penetrated the bay, and it was so badly shot up that longboats had to pull it away to safety. The Americans also sank a gunboat. Several of Arnold's craft were sunk or badly damaged. His Salamis lasted seven hours and was only suspended when darkness fell. The Battle of Valcour Island had been a stand-off, but the Hannibal-turned-Themistocles recognised that if he had to fight a second day, his fleet risked destruction. Then another of those providential fogs rose from the waters. With muffled oars, the survivors of Arnold's flotilla worked as close to the New York shore as they dared and slipped by the British line; daylight found them eight miles beyond it.

The British pursued; ships surrendered or were scuttled. On 14 October, three days after the Battle of Valcour Island, the temporary commodore walked into Fort Ticonderoga. Carleton made some tentative demonstrations in the vicinity but then decided that a siege so late in the season would be unwise. The dismemberment of the colonies would have to wait until the next year. As the naval historian (and rampant Americanist) Alfred Thayer Mahan wrote in what was practically a counterfactual hymn, 'Save for Arnold's flotilla, the British would have settled the business. The little American navy was wiped out, but never had any force, big or small, lived to better purpose.'

If Arnold could inspire the devotion of the men he commanded, and goad them into sacrifice, he could also inspire the dislike of many of his fellow commanders. He could be ruthless in getting what he wanted, savaging those who did not measure up. That might have worked in combat, but behind the lines it cost him dearly. Arnold chose to remain in the field, one biographer has written, 'while detractors played havoc with his reputation'. Instead of being praised for Valcour Island, which may have saved the Revolution, he was blamed for losses of men and ships. At the beginning of 1777, the Continental Congress passed him over for promotion to major general, awarding the rank to lesser men. That galled Arnold; he even considered resigning from the army. Only Washington recognised Arnold for what he was: America's finest fighting general. Finally in May he did receive the coveted promotion.

Arnold was campaigning with Washington in New Jersey when the news came that Ticonderoga had fallen to the British on 6 July. Washington hurriedly sent Arnold northward. The British had initiated what came as close to a grand plan as any set of operational manoeuvres in the Revolution. This time the army of 7,000, including Hessian mercenaries, that sailed down Lake Champlain was commanded not by the over-cautious Carleton but by Major General John Burgoyne, haughty, brave and eager for martial glory. Burgoyne's goal was, again, Albany. Meanwhile a 750-man force led by Lieutenant Colonel Barry St Leger would land on the New York shore of Lake Ontario and make its way east, picking up support in Loyalist settlements along the Mohawk River and joining Burgoyne at Albany. Finally, a significant number of Sir William Howe's army of 25,000 men quartered in the city of New York would sail northward on the Hudson. Once Howe joined with Burgoyne and St Leger, the isolation of New England would be complete. An invasion of the heartland of rebellion was thereafter a foregone conclusion.

We now begin to confront 'What Ifs' small and large. Did Burgoyne really need to waste three weeks building a road through the wilderness? Albany was just a few days' march distant. Did Howe have to ship the bulk of his New York force southward, to capture the rebel capital, Philadelphia, thus weakening the master plan? Lord George Germain, the Secretary of State for the Colonies, had actually drafted a dispatch ordering Howe to move up the Hudson; but in his eagerness to leave London for a weekend in Sussex, Germain put the message aside and then apparently forgot to send it. Howe's decision might have seemed a right one at the time – he did take Philadelphia and handed the Americans some nasty setbacks – but it proved the turning-point for the campaign in the north.

It was at this point that Benedict Arnold became one of the star actors of 1777. When he arrived in Albany, he learned of bloody fighting to the west; St Leger had gained the upper hand and was now laying siege to a Patriot stronghold, Fort Stanwix. He immediately volunteered to lead 900 men on a forced march up the Mohawk River Valley. Luck often favours the opportunist. A Dutch Loyalist named Hon Yost Schuyler was brought into camp, a man who was under sentence of death for recruiting for St Leger. Arnold made a deal with Schuyler, who was thought to be either half-witted or crazy but whom the local Indians regarded as a holy madman. In return for his freedom, he would tell St Leger's Indians that he had escaped from Arnold – who, Schuyler alleged, had brought with him a force of several thousand. (To add a note of authenticity, the Dutchman shot holes through his coat.) The Indians believed him, and melted into the forest, reducing St Leger's force by half. St Leger then gave up the siege of Stanwix and retreated to Lake Ontario. With St Leger in flight and Howe in Philadelphia, Burgoyne was isolated in the wilderness.

Burgoyne had a choice: to retreat, an admission of failure, or to continue on to Albany? Albany it would be. But he suffered another setback when a column of Hessians, detached from his main force to go on a foraging expedition, was destroyed at the Battle of Bennington on 16 August. By early September, when he crossed to the west bank of the Hudson, Burgoyne had fewer than 5,000 combat-ready troops left. The British then began to blunder into American skirmishers. Burgoyne discovered that an American army, which numbered about 8,000 men, was now digging in on a bluff called Bemis Heights overlooking the river. It was a presence he would have to deal with before shouldering on to Albany. The disparity in numbers didn't worry Burgoyne, who had contempt for the fighting abilities of the colonials. His plan was to entrap the Americans – which, given the passivity of their new Northern Department head, Horatio Gates, he might well have done. But that 'if' was negated by the presence of Benedict Arnold, who now commanded the left wing of the American army.

The country where the Battles of Saratoga would be fought was, in 1777, an area of deep maple and oak woods, with occasional clearings where settlers had established farms. (The battles took their name from a nearby village that is now called Schuylerville.) From heights like Bemis, there was a pleasing prospect of distant mountains and, closer up, the Hudson, darkly tranquil and narrowing here as it approached its source. It was around one of the rough log farmsteads, called the Freeman farm, with a stump-littered field some 350 yards long, that the two armies collided on 19 September.

Gates, a shambling, near-sighted man with stringy grey hair, who had risen to major in the British army, was reluctant to fight. Arnold took the initiative. Firing from the cover of the woods, his men battered the redcoat lines drawn up in the open. But when the Americans attacked, they were in turn beaten back. All afternoon there were charges and counter-charges. Riding along his line, waving his sword in encourage-ment, Arnold seemed to be everywhere. When he began to sense that the British were about to give way, he galloped back to Bemis Heights to ask Gates for reinforcements. Gates agreed to send them, but ordered Arnold to remain in camp:

Arnold's rashness, he said, would imperil the army. Instead the Americans, now leaderless, lost their momentum. As darkness fell, the British held the field. Though his troops had suffered fearful casualties, Burgoyne could still claim a measure of victory.

While Burgoyne maintained his position around the Freeman farm and ordered the digging of trenches and the building of redoubts, a different Battle of Saratoga raged. This was the struggle between Gates and Arnold, and its outcome would have a profound effect on the survival of the young American republic. The two generals had started off on friendly enough terms, but their differing styles of command led to an open rift. Arnold had exposed Gates's deficiencies, and Gates plainly resented him for doing so. In his report to the Continental Congress after the battle, Gates did not so much as mention Arnold. Arnold went to Gates's hut and the two men began to shout and insult each other. Gates told Arnold that he was relieving him of command of the left wing. Though Burgoyne little recognised it, his best chance either to win or to escape lay in this rancour between the two Americans. In fact, Gates even contemplated allowing Burgoyne to retire to Canada; he seemed to have no idea of the importance of a major victory to the battered American cause.

Had Burgoyne been tempted to retreat, the arrival of a message from Major General Henry Clinton in New York City persuaded him to stay put. Clinton, who had taken over from Howe, announced that he was about to lead 3,000 men up the Hudson. Clinton did not set out until 3 October. He took a number of Hudson River forts, and his naval vessels easily passed the still-rudimentary fortifications of West Point. (What an advantage he would have rendered his side if he had captured, and held, West Point then.) Burgoyne in the meantime was becoming desperate. He reduced rations and decided to make a large-scale reconnaissance, to probe for weaknesses in the American defences. He admitted that if he did not succeed in 'forcing a passage', he would have to retreat.

The probe commenced late on the morning of 7 October. The woods were aflame with fall colour. Gates and his officers were at mess – the meal was ox heart – when they heard the musket-fire of skirmishers. Arnold rose, and announced he would like to investigate. 'I am afraid to trust you, Arnold,' Gates said. Arnold promised to be cautious. In about half an hour he was back. He reported that the American left was in danger of being rolled up and advised that Gates should send every spare man available. 'General Arnold,' Gates said, 'I have nothing for you to do. You have no business here.'

What if Arnold, a commander without a command, had obeyed?

The booming thud of cannon was added to the crackle of musket-fire; by mid-afternoon, Burgoyne's probe had exploded into a full-blown battle. Arnold could restrain himself no longer. He borrowed a bay horse, swallowed a dipperful of rum from a nearby keg, and rode off toward the sound of the guns. Gates immediately sent one of his orderlies, a Major John Armstrong, to follow on horseback and order Arnold back to his quarters. Arnold simply outran him. One can argue that the course of the war hinged on this horse race.

Arnold took charge. As in the first battle of Freeman's farm, he seemed to be everywhere. He directed the storming of one of Burgoyne's prepared fortifications – named after its commander, the Balcarres Redoubt – but its deep earthworks were too well prepared, too strongly defended. On a nearby knoll there was a second redoubt, the Breymann, and Arnold detected a way to capture that. Under fire, he galloped across the open field and ordered a detachment of American troops to swarm through an empty interval between the redoubts. While he attacked the Breymann from the rear, other Continentals hit it from the front. Resistance disintegrated and the battle was won.

At that victorious point Arnold's luck ran out. One of the retreating Hessians fired at him, killing his horse and putting a bullet in the left leg that had been wounded at Quebec. The horse collapsed, pinning Arnold down and breaking his leg. Only as American troops were pulling their leader from under his mount did Major Armstrong ride up. He had managed at last to overtake the most conspicuous figure on the battlefield.

Six days later, Burgoyne requested a parley with Gates. He was still playing for time, still hoping that Clinton would arrive. He never did, turning back south of Albany. Burgoyne surrendered on 16 October. It was two months before word of the American victory reached Benjamin Franklin and his delegation in Paris. They had the opening that they had sought for so long. France recognised America's independence and agreed to come to its aid with troops and supplies. Had it not been for Benedict Arnold's *rage militair*, would that outcome have been possible? Would the United States have been possible?

How to explain Benedict Arnold's slow drift into treachery? Was it brought on by the months of isolating pain that he experienced after Saratoga? For the rest of his life he would walk with a limp. Or was it the accusations of misuse of his authority for personal gain after Washington made him military governor of Philadelphia in 1778? Or did he simply give up and do what he had been accused of doing since the beginning of the Revolution? Was he turned by his glamorous new wife, the Philadelphia heiress Peggy Shippen? A secret Loyalist, she had once been infatuated with the British officer John André; as Clinton's spymaster in New York, he became her chief contact, as her husband became ever more deeply involved in treason. Peggy Shippen Arnold, we now know, was the highest-paid British spy of the Revolutionary period. Or could it be that Arnold even had idealistic reasons for betraying his country? Did he sincerely believe that the cause that he had nearly died for was doomed and that it was time to effect reconciliation with Great Britain? Whatever the true reason, as early as the spring of 1779, he began, through Peggy, feeding important military information to the other side, and would do so for another eighteen months. Here counterfactual speculation is of little use. It can never completely go inside a person's head. In Arnold's case, his motives will forever remain a mystery.

Washington appointed Arnold to command the left wing of the Continental army in the North. What if he had accepted that command? But Arnold declined, pleading the constantly painful distraction of his unhealed wound. He asked instead to be made Commandant of West Point. Soon after he arrived there, on 4 August 1780, he began to set in motion his scheme to end the war (and to enrich himself in the process). In the three years since Clinton's ships had bypassed it without difficulty, Washington's army had heavily fortified West Point, stringing a chain across the river that effectively blocked traffic. Washington rightly called West Point 'the key to America'. Certainly, its capture would finally realise the British dream, twice frustrated by the man who now sought to betray it, of cutting New England off from the rest of the nation. After a minimum show of resistance, Arnold intended to surrender West Point and its garrison of 3,000 in return for a payment of £20,000.

The year 1780 was, for the American cause, the lowest point of the war. Charleston had fallen. The 'hero' of Saratoga, Horatio Gates, had suffered a calamitous defeat at Camden in South Carolina. Washington's officers threatened mutiny. Public support for the war was waning. Those were setbacks; what Benedict Arnold planned might well have proved fatal.

Arnold and André met only once, for a period of hours on the night and early morning of 21–2 September. Much romantic hogwash has been lavished on André, the handsome young dabbler in art, theatre, poetry – and, one might add, spycraft. He was also the spoiled and arrogant product of his time and class, the lower aristocracy. Like Arnold, he seems to have aspired to great things; both saw West Point was the means to a glorious end.

André had been rowed over from the British sloop-of-war *Vulture* to the west bank of the Hudson; he posed as a New Yorker with the name 'John Anderson'. To make sure that, if captured, he would not be tried as a spy and executed, André wore his red officer's coat under a blue cloak. In a fir grove overlooking the river, the two men cemented their deal; Arnold passed on to André essential details about the strengths and weaknesses of the West Point defences. If Clinton could move fast enough, Arnold apparently said, he might even snare Washington himself, who was due to visit West Point in two days' time. As dawn broke Joshua Hett Smith, Arnold's go-between, interrupted their discussion: it was time to go. From this point the careful plan was beginning to unravel and the 'ifs' to multiply, gradually snaring André in their web.

Arnold's story now becomes André's. Already visibly nervous, 'Anderson' asked to be rowed back to the *Vulture*. But Smith's two tenant farmers, who had rowed him the six miles from the sloop, refused. What if they hadn't? Smith took the general and the major back to his house. Soon after they arrived, they heard an unexpected booming. An American battery on the opposite shore was firing on the *Vulture* and the sloop-of-war was returning fire. Why had the Americans chosen that unlikely moment to initiate an engagement? Smith now refused to risk the water route and the *Vulture* retired down the river to safety. André would have to escape by an overland route. As he was preparing to leave, Arnold handed the young British major safe-conduct passes and a small packet of documents, five out of six of them in his own handwriting. The American told André to put the papers (as he later related) 'between my stockings and feet'. What could have possessed Arnold to act so rashly?

The plans of West Point were useful, but they could also incriminate both men.

Late in the afternoon of the 22nd, André set out on horseback with Smith as his guide. Before they left, Smith insisted that 'Anderson' change his officer's coat for an old claret-coloured one. André did so reluctantly, knowing that if he were apprehended, the disguise would damn him. Smith and André then took a ferry to the other side of the river. It was dark now. An American patrol stopped them, examined the passes, and waved them on. The jovial and loose-lipped Smith was well known, a fool perhaps, but above suspicion. Because of the danger of wandering Loyalist bands, Smith insisted that they spend the night at a nearby farmhouse. They set out the following morning, were stopped by another patrol, and once more waved on. Suddenly Smith announced that he was turning back. 'John Anderson' was now on his own. He had entered the neutral zone between the lines; his mission was nearly complete.

It was near the village of Tarrytown that a group of American militiamen, Westchester County rustics absent without leave and bent on robbing Loyalist travellers, accosted André; one of them grabbed the bit of his horse. Noting that the man wore a torn green-and-red Hessian coat, André assumed that he was close to the safety of the British lines.

'Gentlemen,' he said, 'I hope you belong to our party.'

'What party?' asked the man in the Hessian coat.

'The lower party,' André said, referring to the Loyalists of New York City. He had already said too much, but then he added the words that were to be his undoing. 'I am glad to see you. I am an officer in the British service, and have now been on particular business in the country, and I hope you will not detain me. And for a token to let you know that I am a gentleman –' he pulled out his gold watch.

'Get down,' the man in the Hessian coat said. 'We are Americans.'

They insisted on searching André, forcing him to undress

in a thicket off the road. They went through each garment as he took it off. He stood, finally, naked in his boots. They told him to remove them, too, hoping to find money. They found none. But then they discovered the papers hidden in the stocking. Only the man in the Hessian coat could read. As the naked major stood by, he made a slow and halting examination of the documents.

'This', he exclaimed, 'is a spy.'

As we know, West Point was saved. Benedict Arnold, the Hannibal-turned-Iago, got away – he had himself rowed to the *Vulture*, the same ship that André had been so desperate to return to. Major André, who had not been wearing his officer's uniform and so was liable to the charge of espionage, went to the gallows. On that rough length of hemp hung not just a man, but perhaps the fate of a new nation.

Napoleon Triumphs in Russia

Adam Zamoyski

At the beginning of 1812 the Emperor Napoleon was at the apogee of his power. He ruled directly over some fifty million people, more than half the population of Europe, and indirectly over the Italian and Iberian peninsulas and most of Germany and Poland. On 24 June 1812 Napoleon invaded Russia, at the head of the greatest army ever seen. But less than six months later, on 7 December, he furtively recrossed the Russian frontier, travelling incognito and attended by no more than half a dozen men. His *Grande Armée* was annihilated. Although he managed to raise more troops, and in spite of some brilliant generalship, he was unable to reassert his dominion or hold off the growing coalition deployed against him. On 6 April 1814 he was forced to abdicate and, after an attempted comeback, decisively defeated by the British and Prussians at the battle of Waterloo and incarcerated on the remote island of St Helena. It could have been otherwise.

Napoleon had never intended to invade Russia, let alone conquer it. All he wanted was to make Alexander observe his side of the bargain they had struck at Tilsit in 1807. Then, a defeated Alexander had sued for peace and been given what appeared to be very generous terms. Not only did Napoleon not demand any cession of territory, he actually gave Russia a slice of Poland. All he demanded in return was that she adhere to the Continental System, the blockade aimed at destroying British trade.

The Tsar knew the alliance with France was unpopular, particularly among the traditionalist nobility – one of his courtiers warned that he might end up sharing the fate of his father and grandfather, both of whom had been assassinated.

As the observance of the blockade began to tell on the Russian economy, the alliance became politically unsustainable. Napoleon tried to sweeten the pill by assenting to Russia's invading Sweden and annexing Finland. In 1809 he gave Alexander another slice of Poland. But the Tsar could only justify continued adherence to the alliance if he could acquire the whole of Poland, to which Napoleon would not agree. Towards the end of 1810 Alexander began a relentless build-up of forces along his western frontier.

Napoleon, who needed to go to Spain to conduct the campaign against Wellington in person, feared that these would be launched into Poland and Germany the moment his back was turned. He decided to cow Alexander back into submission. He assembled over half a million men, drawn from as far afield as Spain, Portugal, Naples and Croatia as well as from France, and deployed them against Russia in the spring of 1812. He himself left Paris on 9 May, travelling through southern Germany and stopping at Dresden. He spent the next two weeks holding court there, attended by the Emperor of Austria, the King of Prussia and most of the reigning princes of Germany, a display of power meant to intimidate Alexander.

Alexander had also left his capital for his headquarters at Vilna in Lithuania. His army was numerically strong, but its commanders were no match for the French. He had no allies. He was still embroiled in a war with Turkey in the south, and it seemed likely that in the north the Swedes would take the opportunity provided by a French invasion to recover Finland. On 18 May Napoleon's special envoy, the Comte de Narbonne, arrived in Vilna. He indicated that Napoleon was prepared to make far-reaching concessions in order to keep the alliance going. But the Tsar had come to believe that it was his duty to liberate Europe from Napoleon and, fortified by a religious sense of destiny, challenged him to withdraw his armies from Germany. Napoleon responded by invading. He crossed the River Niemen on 24 June and occupied Vilna four days later. The French forces advanced rapidly, preventing the Russians from concentrating, and it was not until Smolensk, the first city of Russia proper, that an attempt was made to halt the invaders. But after two days' savage fighting, the Russians were obliged to retreat once more.

Alexander appointed a new commander, General Mikhail Ilarionovich Kutuzov, who gave battle at Borodino, seventy-five miles from Moscow. In the bloodiest day's fighting until the first day of the Somme in 1916, the Russian army lost half of its effectives. Napoleon grandly called his victory the Battle of the Moskowa, but it had been a pyrrhic one. He had lost over 25,000 men and most of his cavalry, while the Russians, decimated as they were, had not surrendered. Kutuzov withdrew through Moscow, and then veered round to march back round the south of the city to take up positions in a fortified camp at Tarutino, with his supply bases of Tula and Kaluga behind him.

Napoleon reached Moscow on 14 September, but most of the 270,000-strong population had left in the past few weeks, and there was nobody of rank to surrender the city to him. To make matters worse, the Russian governor of Moscow had given instructions for the city to be fired, and his incendiaries, aided by a strong wind, ignited a fire that lasted four days and devastated up to eighty per cent of the city.

One of Napoleon's chief gifts was an ability to make a quick appraisal of any situation and act fast on it. But in this instance, he lapsed into a lethargy of indecision. He wasted five weeks in Moscow, at the end of which he had no option but to leave. He had not planned the withdrawal, which quickly became a disorderly retreat, and he was caught on the march by the Russian winter, which destroyed his army and led inexorably to his downfall. If only he had behaved with the logic and consequence with which he usually acted, events would have taken a very different course:

As he watched the fire spread across the city from the terrace of the Kremlin, Napoleon realised that he had miscalculated. He had thought that, sooner or later, Alexander's nerve would break and he would sue for peace. Napoleon would be magnanimous. He had even considered giving Alexander the whole of Poland, if only he would help him bring Britain to her knees, and he had a plan for a joint Franco-Russian overland expedition to India. But Alexander and the Russians had been a disappointment. 'How can one make war on people such as these!' he exclaimed to Marshal Berthier as he watched the flames. 'They're barbarians. The only thing to do with them is to push them back into the northern wastes.'

As soon as the fire died down, he prepared to move out. The wounded were evacuated to bases in Poland and Prussia, along with the military stores taken in Moscow and the imperial Russian regalia and booty Napoleon had found in the Kremlin. They were escorted back down the Smolensk road by General Junot's 8th Corps, composed mainly of Westphalians, and Prince Jozef Poniatowski's 5th Polish Corps, both of which were in poor shape and in need of rest.

On 26 September Napoleon marched out with the 4th Corps of Prince Eugène de Beauharnais, Marshal Davout's 1st and Ney's 3rd, as well as his Guard, some 75,000 men in all, leaving the Young Guard in Moscow under Marshal Mortier. He marched south, making for Kutuzov's camp at Tarutino. The Russian army, down to no more than 50,000 men and very short of officers, was in no position to give battle. It fell back in disorder, harried by the French. Napoleon occupied Tula and Kaluga, where he plundered the military stores and destroyed Russia's principal arms factories before moving on. 'Since *messieurs les barbares* are so keen on burning their cities, we must help them!' he quipped to Marshal Berthier. He sent orders to Mortier to blow up the Kremlin and withdraw to Smolensk, and he too turned westwards.

On his way back, he routed a Russian army under Admiral Chichagov, 60,000 men who were covering the Ukraine. He then made for Minsk, where he had built up a large supply depot in the course of the summer. By 13 October, when the first fall of snow covered the ruins of Moscow, the *Grande Armée* was settling into winter quarters around Minsk, with forward positions at Smolensk, Polotsk and Vitebsk. Napoleon set up his headquarters at Vilna. 'The campaign of 1812 is over,' he announced. 'The campaign of 1813 will accomplish the rest!'

In mid-November, he proclaimed the restoration of the kingdom of Poland. He had originally thought of taking his brother Jerome off the throne of Westphalia and making him King of Poland, but Jerome hated the idea, and the Poles despised him. He considered his brother-in-law Joachim Murat, currently King of Naples, for the job. But Murat was too stupid and unaccountable. Some suggested Poniatowski – he was, after all, the nephew of the last king of Poland. In the end Napoleon settled on Marshal Davout, Duke of Auerstädt and Prince of Eckmühl, one of the most faithful of his generals. Davout was a fine soldier and a strict disciplinarian, and if anyone could lick the difficult Poles into shape it was he. He was popular with them and he was also a nobleman, which helped, as most of Napoleon's entourage had execrable manners and were hardly up to fulfilling the role.

Napoleon went back to Paris for Christmas. He had originally intended bringing his Empress, Marie-Louise, to Vilna and importing the actors of the *Comédie Française* to help entertain his court through the winter months. But he thought better of it. 'With the French as with women, one should never stay away too long,' he said to his Master of the Horse, General Armand de Caulaincourt. He spent the three winter months in Paris, raising more troops for the forthcoming campaign, which he hoped would be his last. 'We are getting old, my friend,' he had recently said to General Vandamme. 'We have to finish the business while we still have the strength.'

He left Paris on 15 April 1813. He stopped in various

German capitals in order to flatter and dominate his allies and vassals. In Warsaw, on 3 May, he superintended Davout's coronation. (The occasion was marred for him by the nagging of his Polish former mistress, Maria Walewska, who had wanted to play a prominent role and wished to be guaranteed a preferential position at court.) By 9 May he was back at Vilna, drawing up plans for the next campaign.

Alexander had not been idle during this time. He had persuaded Sweden, with which he had concluded an alliance in the summer of 1812, to provide him with an auxiliary corps. He had also signed an alliance with Britain, but while this yielded money and a quantity of muskets and rifles, the British were unable to spare any troops as they were embroiled in war with the United States of America as well as in the Iberian peninsula. Alexander also mobilised anti-French patriots from all over Germany, who formed a German Legion to fight at the side of the Russians.

In Russia, a mass levy produced nearly 350,000 men. Some were used to fill the gaps in the regular forces, the rest were put through rudimentary training and organised as a militia, uniformed in grey Russian blouses with a cross on their caps and the inscription: 'God and the Tsar'. Alexander's increasingly biblical appeals for the defence of the faith and the fatherland were answered by patriotic noble volunteers, as well as by Cossacks, Bashkirs, Kalmucks and others from the recesses of the empire.

Realists argued that Russia could not hope to win the coming campaign, and that the strain burdening the structure of the state, put in place by Peter the Great only a hundred years before, would destroy it. Noble landowners also feared that there would be no sending the serfs back to work after they had learnt to fight in defence of their land. Others feared social revolution. All this lent support to the peace party, grouped around the former Foreign Minister Count Nikolai Rumiantsev and the Tsar's younger brother Grand Duke Constantine. But Alexander was unshakeable in his resolve.

The only regular Russian forces that had survived 1812 were the remnants of Kutuzov's and Chichagov's armies in the Ukraine, now under Kutuzov, and General Wittgenstein's army which had been hovering on Napoleon's northern flank. This was now based at Pskov, covering the approaches to St Petersburg. It consisted of 80,000 regulars supplemented by 120,000 militia and Cossacks, 25,000 Swedes and the 15,000-strong German Legion. It had over 600 guns of all calibres. Alexander had considered asking his ally the Crown Prince of Sweden, otherwise known as Marshal Bernadotte, to command this, but in the pervasive xenophobic climate he thought it better to appoint General Piotr Petrovich Konovnitsin, a mediocre commander who had managed to cut a dash during the 1812 campaign and affected a trad-itional Russian image. Kutuzov's army, based in northern Ukraine, now consisted of 60,000 regulars, 40,000 militia and 35,000 Cossacks and Bashkirs. Its task would be to strike into Poland as soon as Napoleon's main forces commenced their attack on Konovnitsin, thereby threatening the French army's rear.

On 15 June Napoleon launched his offensive. A body of cavalry 35,000-strong, under Murat, swept up through Latvia, leaving Konovnitsin's main forces on its right flank, and making for Narva. Another corps of 45,000 men under Prince Eugène de Beauharnais marched out in a north-easterly direction to cut the Moscow–St Petersburg road near Novgorod, thereby outflanking the Russians in the east. In the centre, Napoleon himself, with a force of 180,000 men, unleashed a frontal assault on Konovnitsin's army.

The Russians had dug in along an extended line and resisted the French attacks with stoical heroism. They were out-manoeuvred by the French, but even when the line was breached they fought on, with pikes and bayonets, and even with musket-butts and fists. The French had to hack their way through companies of hymn-singing militia determined to die rather than surrender. The battle raged for two days and the carnage was unprecedented. Since the Russians went on fighting as they fell back, an area of over ten square miles was littered with corpses. These were never counted, and losses could only be estimated.

Alexander, who had joined the army at the start of the campaign, was in the thick of the action during the whole of the first day, and many thought that he was seeking a glorious death. Towards the end of the second day, when the Russian positions had been breached and many of the units forced to fall back, Konovnitsin and Alexander were cut off along with their escorts. Determined to avoid being captured, they tried to fight their way out of the encirclement. Konovnitsin was killed in the attempt, and many thought they saw the Tsar fall too. In effect, he had broken through. Accompanied only by a couple of aides-de-camp, he fled from the battlefield in an easterly direction, slipping between French detachments.

The appearance of Murat's advance guard at Narva, only eighty miles from St Petersburg, followed by reports of Prince Eugène's capture of Novgorod, caused panic in the capital. The peace party swelled and everyone began to mutter against Alexander. When news of his death on the battlefield reached the city, Constantine took charge and despatched a messenger to Murat's headquarters proposing an immediate armistice.

Alexander had managed to slip through and reached Tver, the residence of his sister Catherine, an ardent patriot. She exhorted him to rally what was left of his forces and retire into Siberia to continue the fight from there. But he was a broken man. He had been defeated and forced to flee from the battlefield at Austerlitz in 1805, and he felt the humiliation of this second flight all the more keenly. He had always dreamed of emulating the great Russian hero Alexander Nevsky, who had routed the Teutonic Knights in 1242 near the very spot of the last battle, but the Almighty had decreed otherwise, and Alexander submitted to what he believed to be His will. He left Tver on his own, dressed in simple clothes, announcing that he would join a monastery in some remote region.

Although he had destroyed the main Russian army, Napoleon had suffered huge losses outside Pskov, and his men were shaken by the intensity of the fighting. Among the dead was Marshal Ney, 'the bravest of the brave', who had only recently been granted the title of 'Prince de la Moskowa' for his part in the battle of Borodino. Napoleon had had only sketchy news from Murat and Prince Eugène, so he paused for a couple of days following the battle. But then he heard that Kutuzov had been defeated by a combined Polish and Austrian army under Davout. He ordered the advance, and as he closed in on St Petersburg he was met by Murat and attended by Grand Duke Constantine. He entered the Russian capital in triumph on 29 June. He installed himself in the Winter Palace, where he dictated the terms of the peace and of a new alliance.

Russia renounced her Polish and Baltic conquests, along with Finland which reverted to Sweden. Bernadotte, who had fallen into French hands in St Petersburg, was court-martialled and shot as a traitor to France. The Swedes accepted in his place Napoleon's nominee Prince Jozef Poniatowski. Napoleon detached Russia's Ukrainian provinces and created a Cossack state, the Grand Hetmanate of the Ukraine, to be ruled from Odessa by Murat, who became 'Grand Hetman'. The Russian fleet passed under French control, permitting Napoleon to confront the Royal Navy in the eastern Mediterranean and to exclude it from the Baltic altogether, denying it the essential supply of hemp and other ships' stores.

On 15 August 1813, his forty-fourth birthday, Napoleon personally crowned Constantine in an imposing ceremony in the Cathedral of Our Lady of Kazan. He then left St Petersburg for Paris. He was followed by a vast wagon-train bearing most of Russia's gold reserves and, a few weeks later, by a contingent of 15,000 Russian infantry and 20,000 Cossacks, who were to fight under French command in Spain.

As he passed through Berlin he paused just long enough to draw up and sign a decree abolishing the kingdom of Prussia and demoting Frederick William to the rank of Grand Duke of Brandenburg. By the time Napoleon had returned to Paris, reorganised his forces and begun planning the campaign to pacify the Iberian peninsula, Britain, which was now completely isolated, indicated that she was prepared to negotiate. Napoleon responded quickly. Although he would have welcomed the opportunity to defeat that 'sepoy general' Wellington, he was feeling tired, and the prospect of protracted operations in Spain was not inviting. He agreed to an immediate armistice on the basis of a mutual evacuation of the Iberian peninsula and convoked a congress to Paris which would settle the affairs of Europe comprehensively.

'We must have a European legal system, a European appeal court, a common currency, the same weights and measures, the same laws,' he said to his police chief Joseph Fouché,' I must make of all the peoples of Europe one people, and of Paris the capital of the world.' He strutted about the room in which the delegates of every state were assembled, explaining that he had never wanted power for himself, and lecturing them on the benefits he had brought to the areas under his rule.

The Congress of Paris turned most of mainland Europe into a great confederation of semi-sovereign states bound by a common legal system, the *Code Napoléon*, homogeneous weights and measures, and a common currency, as well as by a number of conventions regulating relations between them. The Confederation of Europe was dominated by the French Empire, both by its size and wealth, and by the fact that all its central institutions, its supreme court and its administrative organs were based in Paris. The tone was set at the outset, when every crowned head in Europe had to come to the French capital for the inaugural ceremonies. Napoleon relished his role as host, missing no opportunity to patronise them. In 1824, on the tenth anniversary of the

Congress of Paris, the Confederation was renamed the Empire of Europe, and Napoleon was solemnly crowned in the new Temple of Europe built especially on the Champ de Mars. The ageing composer Ludwig van Beethoven was prevailed upon to write an anthem to celebrate a decade of peace and harmony.

The Austrian Empire, reinforced with acquisitions in the Balkans, remained independent, as did Britain and Russia. Britain was allowed to keep Gibraltar, but not Malta or Hanover, and was effectively excluded from European politics. Austria gradually turned itself into a confederation of ethnically based principalities which cohabited rather more harmoniously than those within the Empire of Europe.

Russia went through an unfortunate period of isolation under the unstable Constantine. Rumours that Alexander had not been killed at Pskov ran through the country periodically, and in 1823 a man claiming to be him managed to start a peasant revolt. In 1827 Constantine was assassinated by a group of courtiers and replaced by his younger brother Nicholas. The new Tsar did his best to restore the *ancien régime* in Russia, but it was impossible to prevent tens of thousands of serfs escaping to freedom in the West, and he was faced with the necessity of abolishing serfdom in 1833. After the initial shock of readjustment, this proved a salutary measure, and Russia began to industrialise in the late 1840s, becoming a strong modern power by the 1860s.

Napoleon died in his bed in 1826 and was succeeded by his sickly and somewhat characterless son. France's grip on the Continent weakened, but the system established by the Congress of Paris survived, held together by a vast and growing bureaucracy, a new self-perpetuating aristocracy based in Paris.

As there were no oppressed nations (even Greece had been taken away from the Turks and incorporated into the Empire – with Napoleon's natural son Count Walewski on the throne), the Romantic cult of the nation never progressed beyond the retrieval of folksongs and the reinvention of national dress. The process of rapid industrialisation that began throughout Europe in the 1830s and 1840s did, it is true, give rise to much misery and social unrest, and this was harnessed by a plethora of trades unions and workers' movements such as the Chartists in Britain. They were under-pinned by the theoretical writings of the followers of Babeuf, Saint-Simon and Proudhon, which called for a fairer social order. But the lack of nationalist tensions and the con-comitant absence of large numbers of disaffected freedom-fighters and émigrés meant that no practical political brand of socialism ever developed.

The growing importance of the pan-European admin-istrative bureaucracy marginalised the role of conventional local politics. The rapid rise in standards of living created a consumer culture which bred political apathy, and the ener-gies of the young were channelled into a succession of increasingly bizarre fads and cults spawned by the Romantic movement. Vague doctrines of love combined with abundant consumption of the newly fashionable narcotics such as hashish and opium produced a curious movement in the 1840s which had young people wandering around from one part of Europe to another with flowers in their hair, but their message was incoherent. The movement was nevertheless seen as a threat to the system, and when large numbers of adepts converged on a number of university towns in the spring of 1848, the police stamped it out in a series of ener-getic clampdowns.

The greatest confrontations concerned economic rivalries, attempts at fixing tariffs and getting groups of states within the Empire to ally their interests with those of Russia, Austria, Great Britain or the United States in order to gain preferential trade terms, arrogate the subsidies distributed under a central taxation system, and generally improve the standard of living. In the 1860s a particularly ruthless commissioner from Bran-denburg by the name of Otto von Bismarck attempted to unite all the various states of Germany, which were among the richest in the Empire, to create an economic lobby which he hoped would suck in the rich industrialised areas of north-eastern France and of western Poland, but his venture became so entangled in the red tape that had grown exponentially over the past decades that it was suffocated.

As politics had become little more than a bureaucratic tussle over different ways of achieving the greatest happiness of the greatest number, people of initiative and genius shunned public life. As the rage for regulation made it increasingly difficult even to make money, most enterprising young people left Europe in search of a less ordered life. Countries such as the United States of America, the Empire of Brazil and a number of smaller states in Southern Africa and the Far East benefited greatly, emerging as the dominant economic and cultural centres by the end of the century.

The *Trent* Incident Leads to War

Amanda Foreman

A little before lunchtime on 7 November 1861, the passengers on board the RMS *Trent* were amazed to find themselves being fired upon by a United States warship. The idea that the Federal navy would attack a British mail packet off the coast of Cuba was so outlandish that at first Captain Moir simply raised a British ensign and carried on sailing. Still firing, the USS *San Jacinto* bore down to within 300 yards of the modest little mail boat. At this point Moir reconsidered his response. The *Trent* slowed to a halt as passengers and crew rushed to the deck. Pushing his way through the crowd, Captain Moir leaned over the railings to confront his attackers. 'What do you want?' he shouted. The answer caused uproar among the passengers, the majority of whom were either British or from the South. The *San Jacinto* had come for the two Confederate commissioners, James M. Mason and John Slidell, who had boarded in Havana as passengers for St Thomas. The North had known for several weeks that the South was sending two diplomats, one to France and the other to Britain, to make the case for diplomatic recognition of the Confederacy. But so far the two men had managed to evade capture. It was one of those perverse pieces of luck that Captain John Wilkes, a noted cartographer but one of the least popular or successful officers in the US navy, should be the one to find them.

Wilkes sent over a small US boarding party which was jostled by an angry crowd. Fully conscious of the dramatic moment, Mason announced he would not leave without a struggle. Meanwhile, Slidell's daughter, Matilda, assumed a heroic pose in front of her parents' cabin, and became hysterical when asked to move aside. Taking advantage of the pandemonium, Slidell's secretary entrusted the commissioners' bulging diplomatic bag to the *Trent's* mail agent, who swore to deliver it personally in London. An hour later, Mason and Slidell, and their secretaries, were ensconced in Wilkes's cabin, surrounded by their luggage and several boxes of cigars and sherry thoughtfully sent over by Captain Moir as a parting gift.

News of the capture reached both the North and South about a week later. The warring states erupted in jubilation. To Southerners it was generally assumed that very shortly Great Britain would join their side, the Federal blockade of their ports would be over, and Europe would recognise the Confederate States. To Northerners, the seizure of Mason and Slidell represented both a blow against Britain and a tangible victory against the South. Although the navy had managed to overwhelm Port Royal in South Carolina, the Federal army had lost every significant engagement thus far. Morale was so low that the US Senate was on the verge of setting up what would be called the Joint Committee on the Conduct of the War.

To his immense satisfaction, Wilkes was fêted as a national hero. The Governor of Massachusetts waxed lyrical about his 'illustrious service' to the war. Every newspaper on the east coast supported his action. Gideon Welles, the Secretary of the Navy, issued a public letter of congratulations. The House of Representatives even passed a vote of thanks. Even the normally cautious President Abraham Lincoln became caught up in the excitement.

However, after the initial euphoria people began to wonder how Britain would respond to this insult to her flag. Some even began to express their doubts over the wisdom of provoking a quarrel. Others, including the majority of the Cabinet, adopted an increasingly pugnacious stance against any suggestion of a climbdown. Anthony Trollope, who happened to be visiting Massachusetts, was both appalled by the virulent anglophobia around him and amused by the feverish consultations of law books by otherwise quite sensible people. Since the Atlantic cable had recently failed, America remained in suspense for four weeks.

London learned of the seizure on 27 November. In fact, the Cabinet had known for several weeks of the American search for the Confederate commissioners. The worldly-wise Prime Minister Lord Palmerston had even tried hinting to Charles Francis Adams, the American Minister, that it really wasn't worth the effort since British foreign policy was far beyond the reach of outsiders. The Cabinet had feared there would be an embarrassing incident somewhere off the Channel, involving the Federal and Confederate navies with the Royal Navy reduced, under international law, to being a mere bystander. The stopping of the *Trent* was far worse.

Public opinion, as expressed in the press and on the street, focused on the insult to the nation's pride and honour. In open meetings around the country, Northern supporters found themselves shouted down by their audience. From Scotland to London, most newspapers blamed the entire crisis on the Americans. Southern supporters quickly took advantage of the crisis to increase their support. In London and Liverpool, they printed posters, gave out banners to street hawkers, and pressed miniatures of the Union Jack crossed with the Confederate flag into the hands of hackney cab drivers. Benjamin Moran, Assistant Secretary of the American Legation, had a nasty shock while walking home from work. Turning up the Strand, he saw the Confederate flag flying from the top of the Adelphi Theatre. 'The sight of this base emblem of slavery, treason and piracy made me ill with rage,' he wrote in his diary.

Charles Adams watched the growing outcry with dismay. He knew this was his moment to act but he was hamstrung by the ominous silence from Washington. He waited in vain for instructions from the Secretary of State. 'Mr Seward's ways', he confided to his diary, 'are not those of diplomacy.

Here have I been nearly three weeks without positively knowing whether the act of the officer was directed by the government or not.' Seward had so often threatened to start a war with Britain that, like many British politicians, Adams could not be sure whether the Secretary of State had secretly planned the incident in order to provoke a war. He could discern 'no escape from the alternative of the surrender of the men but a collision, and yet I do not see the way to that surrender'. Fortunately, Adams decided that until he heard to the contrary, his duty was to foster and maintain good relations between the two countries.

But while the Minister tried to buy time in his interviews with the Foreign Secretary Earl Russell, the Cabinet was busily reviewing preparations for war. Russell summed up his colleagues' fears to the British ambassador in France. 'I think now the American Government,' he wrote, 'under the inspiration of Seward will refuse us redress. The prospect is melancholy, but it is an obligation of honour which we cannot escape.' There indeed were Cabinet members who did not accept that the North wanted war, or thought it had the political will to see it through. But Palmerston's distrust of the American political system swayed the majority. He was convinced that even if Lincoln and Seward wanted to release the commissioners, the 'mobocracy' would prevent it. Furthermore, he argued, it was not simply the case that the Crown law officers had pronounced the seizure unlawful. If Britain was seen by the rest of the world to do nothing, her military standing and international prestige would be irreparably damaged.

Knowing that English newspapers would reach American shores faster than diplomatic dispatches, Palmerston relied on *The Times* to convey his message. On 16 December, the North learned that Lord Lyons, the British Minister in Washington, had been instructed to procure the commissioners' release or ask for his passport. Even more ominously, the paper also announced the first of several shipments of troops and arms to Canada. In all, between 12 December and 4 January, Britain sent out over 11,000 fully equipped officers and men, leaving no one in doubt of her intentions.

Yet, ironically, neither country actually wanted war, although both were convinced that it was the other's secret desire. In Britain, the Cabinet's instructions to Lord Lyons reflected its anxiety not to push the Americans into a more extreme position. The somewhat clumsy first draft of the letter to be presented to Seward was revised once by the Prince Consort – almost his last act before his untimely death – and a second time by Palmerston himself. The language was softened and the assumptions behind the letter altered to remove any implication of blame or malice. Russell also explicitly outlined to Lyons the steps he was to take in order to allow Seward as much room to manoeuvre as possible. An apology, he wrote, was less important than the release of the commissioners. Indeed, an explanation would do. Only if Seward failed to respond within the allotted seven days or returned a negative, was Lyons to leave Washington immediately.

Across the Atlantic, throughout December Southern newspapers continued to celebrate their good fortune; and finally Northerners realised the extent to which the Confederacy was placing its hopes on foreign intervention. Even Seward, who at first blustered that the US would 'wrap the world in flames' before giving up the commissioners, began seeking a graceful resolution. The legality of the seizures aside, he saw that the future suddenly looked extremely precarious. The chairman of the Senate Foreign Committee, Charles Sumner, was so concerned that he prepared a set of predictions for Lincoln. Failure to release the commissioners, he wrote, would mean:

(1) instant acknowledgment of the rebel states by England, followed by France; (2) breaking of present blockade, with capture of our fleet; (3) the blockade of our coasts from Chesapeake to Eastport;

(4) the sponging of our ships from the ocean; (5) the establishment of the independence of the rebel states; (6) opening of these states by free trade to English manufacturers ... making the whole North American continent a manufacturing dependence of England.

Although Lincoln still held out hope that they might be able to avoid a confrontation by inviting international arbitration, Seward was among those convinced that Mason and Slidell had to go.

When the Cabinet met on Christmas Day, Charles Sumner came by armed with letters from England, all urging the government to reconsider its position. Seward's task of persuading his colleagues was also made somewhat easier by the conversion of Edward Bates, the Attorney General. Bates recorded in his diary:

I ... urged that to go to war with England is to abandon all hope of suppressing the rebellion . . . The maritime superiority of Britain would sweep us from the Southern waters. Our trade would be utterly ruined and our treasury bankrupt. In short ... we MUST NOT have war with England. There was great reluctance on the part of some of the members of the cabinet – and even the President himself – to acknowledge these obvious truths; but all yielded to the necessity and unanimously concurred in Mr Seward's letter to Lord Lyons after some verbal and formal amendments. The main fear ... was the displeasure of our own people – lest they should accuse us of timidly truckling to the power of England.

Bates neglected to add that his 'obvious truths' were bolstered by the timely arrival of a letter from the French legation. Halfway through the meeting a messenger had arrived with the long-delayed official response from France. The contents dashed any hope that the US might be able to drive a wedge between Britain and France. The North was isolated: the entire diplomatic corps had registered its objections to the seizure. Seward took advantage of his colleagues' disappointment to press a novel argument. Returning the commissioners, he explained with a straight face, would not be a defeat but a victory for America's position on the rights of neutral ships. After all, the war of 1812 had begun in response to the Royal Navy forcibly removing alleged deserters from American ships. The country ought to be pleased by Britain's embrace of the American point of view. Seward's fluid reasoning proved successful both with the Cabinet and the public, and he emerged from the crisis with an enhanced reputation.

A week later, on 1 January 1862, the two commissioners and their secretaries sailed for England on board the warship HMS *Rinaldo*. Contrary to the hopes and fears sparked by their initial journey, their mission to Europe resulted in failure – just as Palmerston had predicted. Their greatest influence on foreign policy had been during their incarceration.

But what would have happened if France's uncompromising response had arrived after the Cabinet meeting? Buoyed by a false hope that it would be Britain who found herself isolated, Seward's colleagues might have prevaricated or decided to invite international arbitration. Either response would have resulted in Lyons leaving for England the very next day. War would have ensued. The question then, and now, is who would have won? Just as informed opinion in the North feared the worst, so too did cooler heads in Britain assume that the war would be prolonged and ruinous. Even the pro-Confederate *Times* warned that the country could not depend on its better-equipped navy since the North had extraordinary maritime resources. Furthermore,

Our adversaries will lose not a moment after the declaration of war in pressing forward the construction and equipment of cruisers and it must be expected that many of these vessels will, as in the last war, elude the blockade and prowl about the ocean in quest of prey

... It is quite possible that while England is ruling undisputed mistress of the waves a Yankee frigate may appear some fine morning off one of our ports and inflict no slight damage upon us.

The current generation of Civil War historians remains divided on the issue. At one extreme are those who believe that the North would have crushed the Royal Navy, destroyed 'the façade of British military preeminence' and rocked 'the foundations of British economic primacy'. At the other are those who predict humiliation for the North and swift independence for the South. The strength of these wildly divergent arguments depends, in part, on how long the war might have continued. Nevertheless, the evidence does suggest its own story, one in which all sides come out the worse for wear – except for the South.

The war would have been fought on several fronts. While simultaneously battling the Confederate states, the North would have to invade Canada, fight a vicious sea-war and, not least, withstand intense pressure from the major European powers. Conversely, Britain would have to defend the Canadian border and its Caribbean possessions, maintain a blockade of the north-east and Pacific coast, and ensure that France remained her ally.

Thanks to Seward's reputation as an anglophobe, London had been anxiously contemplating the problem of Canada's vulnerability for quite some time. Indeed, successive governments had fretted over the defence of North America since 1782. The border was over 1,500 miles long, thinly fortified, and connected by the most basic roads and waterways. In winter, the snow and ice cut off almost all travel and communication. Various defence plans were already in existence, but one calculation remained unchanged: Canada required a minimum of 10,000 regular troops and 100,000 militia volunteers. Military experts did not believe such a force could defeat an invading army, but it might delay the Americans until the Royal Navy came to the rescue. Although no one seriously believed that the North and South would reunite to fight Britain, experts did fear the sheer number of soldiers at the North's disposal. Since Lincoln's last recruitment call the army had grown to 658,000 men. Even before the *Trent* affair, Palmerston had tried to instil in his colleagues a sense of urgency. As a result, by the end of the summer reinforcements had raised Canada's defences to about 5,000 troops and a similar number of militia volunteers.

Once news of the seizure arrived, the Cabinet rapidly set up a war committee to oversee planning and implementation of the campaign. The War Office reckoned that the Americans would attack Montreal and Quebec first, so its strategies concentrated on offensive measures – such as taking Portland in Maine. Over the course of a few weeks, a well-armed force of 11,000 men sailed out in whatever vessel the Navy could spare or lease. The Cabinet had no doubt that Canadians would vigorously resist an invading army, nor did it fear the military prowess of the American recruit. But it knew that Canada had only a slim chance of remaining British. As *The Times* said, 'We can sweep the Federal fleet from the seas, we can blockade the Atlantic cities; but we cannot garrison and hold 350,000 square miles of country.' Victory rested on such wishful negatives as General MacClellan refusing to part with any troops until spring, Confederate activity tying down the majority of Federal troops, a cold winter inhibiting deployment, and states such as Maine turning against the Union.

As for the 'real' war – the war at sea – a breakdown of the Federal and Royal navies at the end of 1861 reveals that each had particular strengths and weaknesses vis-à-vis the other. The Union navy was numerically superior, with about 264 ships in commission. However, the appearance of strength was belied by several crucial factors. Although Rear Admiral Milne's fleet of forty-two ships was small, the Navy had a further 810 ships stationed in various parts of the globe, and – unlike the US fleet, which was an amalgam of wooden vessels hastily converted from private ownership and the merchant marine – these ships were well equipped and mostly steamers.

On the west coast, the numerical advantage was reversed. The US naval presence consisted of precisely six unmodernised and under-gunned sloops. Their territory spanned from Alaska to Chile; while their base on Mare Island, north of San Francisco, consisted of a poorly supplied dockyard. Against this, the British naval contingent of a dozen vessels or so, including five warships, was positively overwhelming. Unfortunately, there was only one coaling station – in faraway Esquimalt in British Columbia – and one serviceable dockyard between Vancouver and Mexico – Mare Island. Rear Admiral Sir Thomas Maitland regarded his advantage as largely a paper one since the real prey would be British shipping, which would be at the mercy of every decent-sized American schooner.

Although the US was in the process of completing its first ironclad, the *Monitor*, the British had already launched the 9,000-ton screw-steamer the *Warrior* – the most technically advanced iron ship in the world – and would shortly launch two more, the *Defence* and the *Black Prince*. In an ocean battle, the *Warrior* would have sunk every ship in the vicinity. Critics like to point out that the *Warrior* was too big and heavy for the shallow waters off the New England coast, let alone the treacherous waters around the Caribbean. But the soon-to-be built US ironclads were only good for shallow coastal and river work.

The US did not have a naval plan against Britain. Rear Admiral Milne, on the other hand, had already put his fleet on alert. Indeed, he reported that 'the ships' companies are in a high state of excitement for war, they are certainly all for the South. I hear the Lower Decks to-day are decorated with the Confederate colours.' His instructions from London were to end the blockade of the Southern ports (without directly co-operating with the Confederacy). How he achieved this was to be his own affair. Milne was one of those officers who justly inspired complete confidence. Clever, determined, resourceful and utterly reliable, he embodied the best qualities of the Royal Navy. The First Lord of the Admiralty, the Duke of Somerset, was quite content to rest the country's hope of victory in his hands.

Milne's strategy depended on a three-pronged attack. One force, under Commodore Dunlop, would sail from Vera Cruz and clear the Federal navy from the Gulf. The larger, Milne's, would attack the US blockading fleet and then proceed up the coast to the north-east where it would establish a blockade of the major northern ports. Unlike the hapless Maitland on the Pacific coast, Milne would be able to count on reinforcements, a sufficient number of coaling vessels, and a working dockyard in Bermuda.

Milne himself thought that his plan had, in the short term, a good chance of success. A mere three months later, however, after the launch of the USS *Monitor*, he felt that the advantage had started to turn in favour of the North and he looked back to the *Trent* affair as Britain's most favourable moment. It is certainly true that most historians who argue in favour of a Northern victory are basing their judgements on future developments in the war. During the next three years the North's industrial capacity would exceed all expectations, its armies grow to a size never before envisaged, its naval fleet become the object of fear and jealousy. But before then the North would have to overcome immediate and possibly insuperable obstacles, and not just in the naval arena.

Although the mere threat of war had sent British financial markets spinning, the US suffered an immediate decline. In London, Lloyd's insurance on shipping to the US rose from five guineas to twenty. Railroad stocks – which accounted for about fifteen per cent of the total values of securities on the London Stock Exchange – dropped sharply, as did the price of consols (government debt). In the North, however, it was not only the exchanges which experienced turmoil. By December the country's antiquated financial structure was on the verge of collapse, creaking under the strain of its dependence on gold reserves; the *Trent* affair lent impetus to its rapid disintegration. Panic among investors led to a freeze on investment and a run on the banks, causing specie reserves to plummet so precipitously that many institutions had to suspend payments. This in turn prevented the US Treasury from being able to raise funds or pay its creditors. On 10 January 1862, a frightened Lincoln admitted that 'the bottom is out of the tub'; the country was all but bankrupt. Fortunately, the financial crisis was resolved through a combination of bold and innovative thinking by Salmon P. Chase, the Secretary of the Treasury, and improved national morale due to some Northern successes in early 1862. But, if Britain had declared war, investor confidence would have continued to plummet all the while as Milne's blockade caused devastation to Northern commerce. Clever tinkering with the financial system would not have been enough to convince lenders to part with their money.

Britain also had the advantage of international support while the US would have found herself isolated by naval blockade and European opinion. Moreover, as Palmerston noted, she also had the benefit of a peaceful moment throughout the Empire, and calm in Europe. The unification of Italy was almost complete, Germany had yet to erupt, the Tsar of Russia was distracted by domestic concerns and France – with its eye on Mexico – had every reason at that moment to remain on good terms with Britain. Unlike the US, Britain did not have to worry about fighting a war on two fronts. The likelihood is that by freeing Southern ports and allowing normal commerce – particularly the export of cotton – to resume, Britain would have made it possible for France and Europe to recognise the independence of the Confederate States.

At that point, Seward's diplomacy would have resulted in the very thing that he and the rest of the country had most feared: the country locked in a double war and isolated commercially and diplomatically from Europe. The acquisition of Montreal and Quebec, plus some frozen waste-land, would have been poor compensation for the permanent division of the Union. As for Britain, her naval victory would have been discounted because of the disparity of strengths, while her military defeat would have been perceived both at home and abroad as a tremendous humiliation. At the very least Palmerston's ministry would have been vulnerable to Conservative attack, and might even have fallen. The structure of US politics would have protected Lincoln, but he would have been under intense pressure to sue for armistice with Britain. In short, if the Trent incident had led to war between Great Britain and the United States, both sides would have lost.

Archduke Franz Ferdinand Survives Sarajevo

Norman Stone

The young terrorists had come, seven of them, over the mountains from Serbia to kill the heir to the throne of the Austrian Empire. For them, young Bosnian Serbs, the Archduke Franz Ferdinand Habsburg was a symbol of oppression. Bosnia had been under the Turks until 1878, when the Austrians had taken it over and ruled it as a colony – pompous public buildings, education, a railway. The capital, Sarajevo, had even become a showcase for the civilisation of Central Europe, featuring cafés with elaborate cakes and the foreign newspapers, superb trains (the arrival and departure of which would be saluted by a proud stationmaster in full-dress uniform), rather grandly built schools where, in starched collars, the sons and daughters of illiterate peasants were encouraged to see themselves as pioneers of a civilised future.

Yet there was this problem: expectation could never match reality, and many of the schoolteachers were full of bile. As a Russian conservative had remarked around this time: 'In Russia, the tavern does less damage than the school.' Teachers' training colleges produced more than their share of animus-ridden nationalists, and in this category were the seven terrorists coming over the mountains in June 1914 – the first echelon of the national liberation fronts that were to become such a feature of the twentieth century.

The terrorists' dream was for a Greater Serbia, to include partly Serb Bosnia. The seven young would-be murderers did their training in Belgrade, where plotters vaguely connected with radical politics wanted to provoke some sort of crisis in relations with Austria. The young assassins were to be their tool in accomplishing this. On 28 June 1914, Archduke Franz

Ferdinand's procession drove into town – for him a statement of the Austrian presence in the backward Balkans. The Archduke, in his blue general's uniform, rather gloweringly saluted. One of the murderers threw his bomb. It missed, bouncing off the back of the car. Another would-be assassin, Gavrilo Princip, a trainee schoolteacher, seeing what had happened, made himself scarce and went to a café on the other side of the river.

The Archduke himself at first made for safety in the governor-general's headquarters where the governor-general, a neurotic homosexual whose career the Archduke had sidelined, had organised for him to be greeted by little girls in national dress offering folklore dances and cakes. In a rage – he was given to rages – Franz Ferdinand found an excuse to move on, and was driven back down the road, on the other side of the river. This time his driver took a wrong turning – as chance happened, straight into the street where Princip was sitting at the café, calming his nerves. The driver, reversing, stalled; Princip saw his target arriving, and fired. But he was nervous, and ducked his head as he did so. A loyal officer, Count Harrach, stood on the running-board, thereby deflecting Princip's aim. The Archduke, wounded in the upper arm, cancelled the rest of his programme and went back to his residence in Vienna, the Belvedere Palace.

The Belvedere had been built two centuries before by Prince Eugène of Savoy, who had led the Austrians victoriously into the Balkan peninsula. Back then it was wild country, and the Austrians had brought civilisation: hygiene, trains, philosophy doctorates, and that oddly shaped lavatory-bowl, designed to avoid nocturnal plopping noises. Behind the net curtains and the potted plants, little girls thumped their way through scales, boys learned their Latin, and the old Emperor's portrait hung on the walls.

However, Austria was weak – so weak that, even for the Archduke, private detectives had had to be hired from Budapest to mingle with the crowds to try to spot would-be assassins. Public money was frittered away in endless penny-packets because there were eleven nationalities in the Empire, and each had to be bought off with jobs and railways and hospitals. In the South Slav lands, of which Bosnia was one, this approach did not solve the nationality problem at all. There were demands for more self-determination, and a growth in terrorism was the result. The terrorists usually found safe bases in Serbia, and by 1914 the Austrian author-ities were losing patience: why *should* they have to put up with such a challenge from a small and inferior state that had grown too big for its boots? The only answer must be to teach the Serbs a lesson.

So when Franz Ferdinand got back to the Belvedere, the Chief of the General Staff, Franz Conrad von Hötzendorf, his own protégé, came and demanded tough action against Serbia. He had called for this before. If things went on as they had done, he said, the Empire itself would fall apart, because other nationalities would also press for independence. Yes, agreed the Archduke, as he, too, had said it all before; but the situation in Europe is very tense indeed. The Serbs had an alliance with Russia; suppose Russia is willing to go to war to protect them? An Austro-Russian war might promote general revolution. The Tsar is our best ally, argued the Arch-duke – we neglected him at the time of the Crimean War and we lost Italy and Germany as a result, because, when the Prussians challenged us to a fight, they had Russia's support. The Archduke agreed that something had to be done about the problem with the South Slavs, but asked for more time.

The Archduke's next appointment was with the Hungarian Prime Minister, Count Tisza, who lost no time in con-gratulating him upon 'Your Imperial Highness's escape from these foul assassins'. He added: 'Your Highness may perhaps be considering punitive action against Serbia, in which case the Hungarian government must ask for its viewpoint to be considered.' (He meant by this that he was against.) Franz Ferdinand did not like Hungarians, finding them too arrogant, especially when, like this one, they were Calvinist Protestants. But he agreed with Tisza: suppose Austrian troops marched into Belgrade, they could hardly stay. The Austrian Empire had enough South Slavs on its hands without taking on Belgrade's Serbs as well: 'Von dieser Sorte hat man schon genug' ('we have enough of that lot'), he said. Tisza and the Archduke agreed: all that could be done was to interrogate the captured assassins and, on that basis, try and get the Serbian government to control its people better.

Franz Ferdinand had his ideas as to how the monarchy's problems might be solved, but here he and Tisza were at odds. Tisza was a sort of Hungarian imperialist, who wanted to take over the South Slav lands and run them from Buda-pest, as had happened in the Middle Ages. By contrast, Franz Ferdinand meant to set up a South Slav kingdom under himself. This meant a breach with the historic arrangements of the Habsburg Empire. Its various parts had old laws and boundaries; interference with them meant endless lawyers bobbing up and down, using the excruciatingly ponderous language of Central European jurisdiction, with reference to impenetrable tomes.

Yet the South Slav lands were very complicated; there were not just Serbs, and Muslim Bosnians, but also Catholic Croats, some of whom strongly identified with Catholic Austria but who were ruled by Protestant or even Jewish Hungarians, who looked down on them and preferred the more direct Serbs. Franz Ferdinand wanted to put Croatian lands together and attach Bosnia to them in a new kingdom, perhaps called 'Yugoslavia' – from the South Slavs' word for themselves. Its capital would be Zagreb and Catholic Croats, not Orthodox Serbs, would be the leading group. Under this scheme the Hungarians would be shown the door. Hungary was far too large, stretching almost from the Black Sea to the Adriatic, and half of her inhabitants did not even use Hungarian as a native language.

Although they would be unlikely to welcome this new

arrangement, the Hungarians might give in to pressure from Germany, if the German Emperor Wilhelm II could be brought to bear. He and the Archduke had met that spring at Franz Ferdinand's estate in Bohemia and they had talked about such things. 'Herr, gedenke der Rumänen,' the German Kaiser had said, in stilted language, do not sacrifice Romanians, who have oil, to the Hungarians, who do not. The fact was that the Austrian Empire could only really be reformed if the privileged position of Hungary were reformed, and especially if Budapest stopped trying to make everyone speak Hungarian. There could then be a proper federation.

As it happened the next visitor to the Belvedere, also bringing good wishes for the Archduke's recovery, was the German ambassador, Baron von Tschirschky. He was not much liked in Vienna: he was a stiff north German of the sort who agreed with Bismarck that 'the Bavarian is a cross between the Austrian and homo sapiens'. He had been reporting to Berlin that Austria hardly counted as a Great Power any longer. Over the past year or so he had been urging caution, and told the more hot-headed anti-Serbs in Vienna that his government would never support some madcap scheme for occupying Belgrade. Now, Tschirschky, too, wanted to know the Archduke's thoughts.

Tschirschky told the Archduke that, while he offered his government's condolences, he must allow himself to suggest that reacting in a moment of indignation, however justified (*berechtigte Entrüstung*) would not be appropriate (*angebracht*) for actions with far-reaching consequences that might involve Berlin. The Archduke agreed. He did not like Tschirschky and his humourless condescension – talking to him, nursing his still-smarting arm, he was somehow reminded that in Austria the trams stank of garlic and the trains were slow. The Archduke would have been personally much happier in the company of Russian reactionaries, but he knew that he needed the Prussians: they alone could lean on the Austrian Germans and the Hungarians. Meanwhile, there must be no upsetting of the Balkan apple-cart, let alone the international system, which had kept the peace these forty years and more.

Tschirschky reported back to Berlin that the Archduke did not want war, that Tisza had also opposed the idea, and that the Hungarian Finance Minister, when asked how long his finances could support a war, had replied three weeks. The Archduke had also indicated to Tschirschky that 'radical measures' must be taken to deal with the whole South Slav problem, but not through war, not until the old Emperor was gone, and only along lines that were acceptable to Berlin. A few days later the Archduke held a small evening party, to which he invited men who, he knew, sympathised with his ideas for radical reform. There was an anti-semitic Romanian poet, Octavian Goga; another Romanian, the journalist Aurel Popescu, who had written a best-seller called *The United States of Greater Austria*, advocating confederation; a Count Czernin, from one of the greatest aristocratic families of the Empire, and a likely future foreign minister; a Slovak journalist called Hodza, who had been in trouble with the Hungarian authorities for his advocacy of Slovak language rights; a young clergyman, Mgr Seipel, who saw salvation in the reinvigoration of the Catholic Church's political role; a Croat nationalist, Josip Frank, who was, as it happened, Jewish. Informal minutes were taken by the Archduke's young political adviser, a Baron von Weidenfeldt-Frauenfels.

The group talked around the table, agreeing that federation must be the answer, that Hungary would have to be challenged, that a central parliament based upon universal suffrage could never work in Austrian circumstances, and that a single political organisation, perhaps called the 'Fatherland Front', might be the answer. The name itself made a good alternative to the otherwise thinkable 'Christian Social', which, Weidenfeldt pointed out, would be a liability since 'Christian' would be taken to mean 'anti-semitic' and 'Social' would simply mean 'stealing'.

One or two of the group were prompted to say, with no offence intended to present company, that there were just too many Jews – too many migrants from the backward Polish–Ukrainian and Hassidic areas (*Ostjuden*) and too many disruptive (*zersetzerisch*) Jewish elements – in the law, in journalism, in left-wing politics, and in department stores that unfairly competed with small shops. Something would have to be done: perhaps a *numerus clausus* in universities and certain professions, they suggested?

The talking went on, as it did in Austria: but there was nothing between daring chatter and apocalypse. In November 1916, when the aged Franz Joseph died, the new Emperor, Franz Ferdinand, wanted to put his programme into action. Pointedly, he delayed being crowned in Budapest. There already was an old plan in the Ministry of War in Vienna, codenamed *Fall 'U'*, dating back to 1905, for the military occupation of Hungary, quite as had happened in 1849. But this time things were different. In the first place, the Croat gambit did not work: the Croats were too divided, those on the Dalmatian coast being mainly republican, while the nobility of the interior regarded their horses as more important than their peasants, and the Zagreb intelligentsia could only sigh: 'God save us from Croatian culture and Serbian bombs'.

The Hungarians, it was feared, would not be easy to defeat (nor had they been in 1849, even after Russian intervention). One of them, a Count Bethlen, came up with an ingenious scheme. The Archduke had made a rather unfortunate marriage, to a woman not of royal birth; his children could not easily inherit the throne. That problem might be got around, suggested Bethlen, if the Hungarian parliament passed the relevant legislation, but of course this could only happen if there were properly constituted royal authority for the counter-signature. Franz Ferdinand therefore accepted coronation and swore the oath to preserve the integrity of Hungary, come what may. Like his predecessors, he sat on horseback on the Mattyas Hill in Buda, and ceremonially

waved his sword to the north, west, south and east in affirm-
ation, though he did it with his characteristic glower as the
grand Hungarian aristocracy tittered about his wife.

The affairs of Central Europe under the Habsburgs therefore just went on and on, without solution, or, rather, on the
expectation that there was none. But Central Europe was
now falling into a wider pattern, for Germany was creating
her own *Mitteleuropa*. One of her prominent liberals, Friedrich
Naumann, wrote a best-seller with that title in 1915. It meant
a sort of Germanic Commonwealth, or Central European
Common Market, running in effect from the northern cape
of Norway through the Balkans and Turkey as far as Baghdad,
where the oil had started to flow. The railway from Berlin to
Baghdad constituted its spine.

The plan made sense, because Germany was economically
dominant and her great cartels wanted to set up a huge
protectionist bloc. Much of Central Europe was just German
in fancy dress, anyhow, argued Naumann – even Russia had
really been set up by Scandinavians whom the Finns had
called 'Ruotsi', their name for Sweden, and Polish civilisation
had fallen off the back of a Teutonic Order wagon. Austria
and Germany fitted together quite easily, and now there was
the further prize of Turkey on offer, together with the oil of
Mesopotamia. All Franz Ferdinand's fussing about Zagreb
looked like a mere detail in the far bigger picture.

It was over this that Germany found herself colliding,
again and again, with Russia. She too had her ambitions.
Constantinople was the crowning piece of the whole Orthodox approach to politics: drive the Turks out, as the Tartars
and Mongols had been driven out, or tamed. Russians dreamt
of Tsar Nicholas II being crowned in the Hagia Sophia, his
warships sailing through the Straits to threaten the Suez
Canal and his armies on the Chinese borders. It would constitute an enormous feat, one to silence any carping liberal
or socialist revolutionary.

Of course all of this had remained a pipe-dream until

quite recently. Until around 1880 Russia had counted as backward – a large population, yes, but illiterate and mainly rural (and not very good at being rural). Furthermore, there were not enough railways to carry forces with any speed to take part in a European war. German military planners therefore thought that, with their far superior railways – the Cologne bridges alone could take more trains in a commuting evening than the Russian railways could manage to send to Poland in a working week – they could tackle France in a war and knock her out before the Russians appeared at Königsberg in East Prussia, let alone at Berlin.

Yet by 1916, all of these 'givens' were changing. Russia was not backward any more; she had been growing at an extraordinary rate and had become the greatest of 'emerging markets'. One only need look at the buildings of St Petersburg or Kiev to appreciate this transformation. What had caused the boom? Foreign investment, especially French, had mattered initially, but with the gold standard Russia had trustworthy money at last, and her trade also grew with better railways and canals. In Edwardian England, they ate Siberian butter. Smokestacks grew, so did electricity, and so did Russian prowess in invention: an award-winning lorry in 1910, the best aircraft design (Sikorsky in Kiev, who emigrated), the most advanced radio technology.

In 1912 the German Chancellor, Theobald von Bethmann Hollweg, visited Russia and was deeply impressed and by 1914 Russia was generally viewed as the coming power. In 1913, this was reflected in grants of money for armaments – 'the Great Programme' – and for railways which, in wartime, would allow soldiers and guns to be moved to the front far faster than ever before imaginable. Russia would now have more guns than Germany. In the past, a growing Russia would not have greatly alarmed Berlin; the two had co-operated and were often run by men of similar background, Baltic aristocrats whose names goose-step across the page: von der Ropp, von Manteuffel-Zoege, von der Pahlen, Graf von Uxkull-Gyllenbandt and so forth. But now it was different. The Baltic Germans had either gone native or dropped out. Besides, Russia was allied with France, and French public opinion, strongly nationalist since 1871, might easily be swayed towards war against Germany.

By 1914 the German High Command had started to panic. The generals said that if the Russian railway programme were completed, as was planned by 1917, then Germany with five million men under arms would have no chance of winning, because the Russian and French armies – with five million men each – would reach the German borders at more or less the same time. In 1914, whenever members of the German Establishment met, the talk was of 'war before it's too late'. On 8 July Bethmann Hollweg said as much to his private secretary, Kurt Riezler, as they sat on the terrace of his country house in Brandenburg after dinner. 'Russia grows and grows, and weighs upon us, like a nightmare,' he remarked, and Riezler wrote it all down in his diary. In other words, 1914 smelt 1945 in the air. Bethmann Hollweg even told his son, who proposed planting elms, that there was not much point since because they took so long to grow, only the Russians would profit.

Such was the mood in Berlin, especially after the reverses of 1913 and 1914. The Franco-Russian alliance had become stronger, and the British were drawing closer to it. The Germans diagnosed *Handelsneid* (trade envy) and they were not wrong since they were eating into British markets.

Russia's strength started calling into question the future of the Ottoman Empire. In spring 1914 the Russians used the pretext of protecting Christian minorities to push through an unequal treaty, giving them a protectorate over eastern Anatolia, which was partly Armenian. The French were after Syria, the British, Mesopotamia, while the mood in Berlin was desperate. When news of the attempted murder of the Archduke came through, that boiling hot summer, and the Austrians sent a message asking if a special envoy, a Count

Hoyos, could come and discuss what should now happen, the Germans were indeed casting about for some excuse to provoke the Russians.

Bethmann Hollweg suggested to Hoyos that the attempt on the Archduke might be used profitably: why not send a very sharply worded note to the Serbian government, accusing it of complicity in terrorism and threatening (by implication) war? Behind the scenes, the Chiefs of the two General Staffs, Moltke and Hötzendorf, were exchanging informal messages suggesting that maybe the time was right.

Hoyos went back to Vienna and put the Germans' proposal on the Cabinet table, but Archduke Franz Ferdinand and Count Tisza had it turned down flat. In Admiral Tirpitz, the architect of the German navy, they had a powerful ally in Berlin. He simply did not want to risk a war; if Great Britain came in, he argued, the German navy would be too weak to challenge the Royal Navy so it was best for Germany to stay out. Besides, there was a majority in the Reichstag for the Social Democrats, the anti-clerical Democrats and the Catholic Centre Party. Turning them into a governing coalition was difficult, or even, short of a crisis, impossible. But none favoured aggressive war; in fact they would only support finance for the military at all on the grounds that the burden would force the government to introduce a serious direct tax on the rich.

So, with some grumbling in Vienna and Berlin, the crisis of July 1914 failed to turn into anything more than that. The Austrians sent Serbia a severe note, with demands that were 'harsh but not unacceptable'. The Russians instructed their allies to give way. Belgrade promised to crack down on terrorist cells, had a couple of army officers court-martialled, and formally told the Austrians they would inform them if they heard of any more plots.

Bethmann Hollweg (and everyone else in 1913) had been right about Russia: she was indeed becoming a superpower. Her Great Programme did indeed permit her to appear with several armies on the German and Austrian borders within three weeks of the outbreak of any war, so the German generals were therefore a force for caution by 1916. There does, after all, come a point in any elderly general's career when the ambition to have a square named after him gives way to concern about his pension. Pensions were now winning in Potsdam.

The central problem was that although Germany was immensely strong, she had been doing too much in simultaneously building a High Seas Fleet strong enough to scare the British and maintaining an army large enough to take on France and Russia. She could not do both, the more so as her finances were in a mess. Germany was a federal country, with too many spending-points. The most active of the younger staff officers, a Colonel called Ludendorff, stated that the country could not now risk a war; the admirals and politicians, he said, must now drink 'die Suppe, die sie uns eingebrockt haben' ('the brew, that they have stewed up for us').

The next great crisis occurred over the Ottoman Empire. By virtue of the unequal treaty forced through in the spring of 1914 (and ratified at the end of the year), the Russians had a right even to garrison some places in eastern Anatolia. 'The Turks were almost helpless, their towns filling up with hundreds of thousands of stricken refugees from the Balkans and the Aegean islands taken by Italy or Greece. The Arab provinces were beginning to stir, and in Yemen there was a full-scale revolt. Taking advantage of this, Armenian revolutionaries ('Dashnaks') staged a provocation by blowing up the branch office of the Ottoman Bank in Trabzon. Their own Patriarch protested, in a sermon at the Kum Kapi Cathedral in Istanbul, as one of his predecessors had done twenty years before. He said that Turks and Armenians had lived together for a thousand years, that nowhere in Anatolia were Armenians a majority of the population, and that the Orthodox, Russians and Greeks were no friends to the schismatic

Armenians. The nationalists, goading the Turks, would only bring about the ruin of the Armenian nation, in other words.

As had happened in 1899, the nationalists shot the Patriarch; as had happened in 1896, enraged Turks set about harmless Armenians; yet as had not happened in 1896, the Great Powers decided to intervene. Russian warships anchored opposite the Golden Horn, and, in the Black Sea, at Sinop, sank the weaker Turkish vessels. Russian troops, with an Armenian legion in tow, occupied towns of eastern Anatolia, and made for the Kurdish areas of Mesopotamia, where, at Mosul, oil had been discovered.

Here, in summer 1916, was the crisis that Bethmann Hollweg had foreseen in July 1914, or at any rate a version of it. But since Russia was now strong, there was no chance of a rerun of the Crimean War. A second congress was held, in Berlin, to sort out the Eastern Question. The earlier congress, in 1878, had been dominated by Bismarck and Disraeli but this one was dominated by Sazonov, the Russian Foreign Minister, and Sir Edward Grey. Between them, they held the trumps. The Ottoman Empire was partitioned between Russia and Great Britain, Germany left with vague guarantees regarding the Baghdad railway and access to markets. Russia could realise her old dream, and at the same time do herself a very good turn, commercially, by taking over Constantinople, now called Tsargrad.

As she had shown in Central Asia, Russia was quite skilled at handling Muslim rulers and clergy. The Sultan was moved to honourable residence in the old Ottoman capital, Bursa, and central Anatolia remained Turkish. Greeks and Armenians, as clients of the British and Russians, took the western and eastern parts, though both, in time, faced a tough Turkish resistance, which wore them down. The British took the Arab areas, and much of the oil.

In other words, Germany had lost, without fighting. She was driven back onto her core, *Mitteleuropa*, which she could build up as a powerful economic bloc, quite along Naumann's lines. One of the more statesmanlike politicians, Gustav Stresemann, suggested that the time had come for a unification of the war-torn continent, and he found willing listeners in Paris. For it was the French who had lost most. In the partition of the Ottoman Empire, they got very little – a scrap or two in the Lebanon – but there were wise Frenchmen who had a strategy to cope. The French had missed out on the population growth that had doubled or trebled the size of other European countries. They also had the least industry, and half of them lived in places with fewer than two thousand inhabitants. In a way, the resilience of peasant agriculture – the root cause of this – was the revenge of Louis XVI: 'Liberty, equality, fraternity' had made the small peasant the master of France, and the last thing he wanted was children to feed. As Madame de Staël had said, Germany must be the model – 'inspirons-nous de l'Allemagne' – the Athens of Europe.

Édouard Herriot, the mayor of Lyons and a prominent radical politician, was also an expert on Kant, and knew Germany. He could see that, given German domination of Europe, France must simply find a way of joining her in an economic bloc – one that would put French iron ore together with German coal in a Coal and Steel Community, based on steel-rich Luxemburg. Lyons was the most industrially advanced part of France, with electricity associated with the Rhône. Joseph Caillaux, a right-wing politician with strong industrial connections, became Prime Minister, and put this programme into action.

Herriot and Caillaux arrived in Berlin just as the congress broke up, and talked of co-operation between metallurgical concerns. Co-operation with *Mitteleuropa* meant the end for French ideas of greatness, of continental domination, and of a world role beyond a cultural one. But if, in Germany, there were new Ottonians, what could France do, beyond relapsing into the world of Charles the Simple and Louis the Fat? Experience showed that Frenchmen only made babies when they lost illusions. Now, they started to make babies again.

Lenin is Assassinated at the Finland Station

Andrei Simonovich Robertski

[An extract from chapter seven of Robertski's *Kerensky's Triumph: The Russian Revolution and Its Aftermath*, published in New York, Petrograd and London in 1967. Note: The Julian calendar was maintained in Russia until January 1918, when the Kerensky government introduced the Gregorian version in line with the rest of Europe. Robertski uses the Old Style until that date and the New Style thereafter.]

The assassination of V. I. Lenin at Petrograd's Finland Station a few minutes before midnight on Monday 3 April 1917 might not seem like a seminal moment in the development of the Russian Revolution, but at that time he was a well-known Bolshevik agitator and polemicist who was in essence the unacknowledged leader of the Party. It seems clear from his *April Theses*, written on the train that took him from his long exile in Switzerland back to Russia via Sweden and Finland, that Lenin was planning radically to alter Bolshevik strategy towards the Provisional Government. For that reason his assassination poses one of the fascinating What Ifs of History, so beloved of those strange counterfactual historians whose parallel-universe essays are published from time to time.

Imagine a world, if it is possible, in which Lenin was *not* shot dead as he began to address the welcoming crowd at the Finland Station, but instead went on to put his tremendous energy, eloquence and polemical abilities into attempting to overthrow Prince Lvov's Provisional Government in 1917. Today, instead of the liberal democracy that Russia has enjoyed for the past half-century, a creed called Marxism–

Leninism might well have extended across much of Russia and Eastern Europe, and perhaps even so far as the Far East.

Yet before I posit anything too far-fetched, let us consider what did in fact happen. The abdication on 2 March 1917 of Tsar Nicholas II in favour of his brother Michael, who the following day renounced the throne as well, brought the rule of the Romanov dynasty to an end after three centuries. In its place was established the uneasy dual authority of two distinct bodies. The first was the Fourth Duma's Leaders' Committee which soon became the Provisional Government and took on executive authority in the state. The second was the Petrograd Workers' and Soldiers' Soviet, a body designed to protect the interests of the Russian proletariat. Both bodies were housed in the magnificent Tauride Palace, and although the Provisional Government initially had the upper hand, a power struggle between the two was always a possibility.

Under the presidency of Prince Georgi Lvov (who also took the Interior portfolio), the Provisional Government arrayed a broad spectrum of liberal, constitutional monarchist, moderate, and also socialist opinion. Its leading lights included A. I. Guchkov, the Moscow landowner and industrialist who was Minister for War, Pavel Milyukov, a history professor and constitutional monarchist who became Minister for Foreign Affairs, M. I. Tereshchenko at the Finance Ministry, and most prominently Alexander Kerensky, the firebrand socialist orator who took the Justice portfolio. Kerensky had been the darling of the Russian working classes ever since he had resolved a bloody conflict in the British-owned Lena goldfields four years earlier, to the great satisfaction of the oppressed goldminers there.

It was Kerensky who very early on appreciated that if he could prove to the Russian proletariat that the Provisional Government, rather than the Petrograd Soviet, truly represented their best interests he could avoid the danger of a violent struggle between the two bodies for ultimate power.

Prince Lvov's was a broad-based coalition made up of talented and, as it turned out, far-sighted politicians who were willing to submerge their personal ambitions in order to succeed in the wider task of ensuring that their bloodless, essentially bourgeois, revolution was not followed – as it easily could have been – by a violent proletarian one.

Just across the hall of the Tauride Palace sat the Petrograd Soviet, itself also a coalition. Mensheviks, Socialist-Revolutionaries and Bolsheviks formed the major constituent parts of this body of workers' and soldiers' representatives. Each factory and army battalion in the city and each naval vessel in the port sent a delegate to the Petrograd Soviet, dozens of sister organisations of which were being founded all over Russia. Since the split between the Bolsheviks (*bolsinstvo* = 'majority') and the Mensheviks (*menshinstvo* = 'minority') at the Second Congress of the Social-Democratic Party in a London church hall in 1903, the two factions had adopted entirely different methods of trying to bring about their common dream of a Marxist utopia. Since the March Revolution, however, they had nevertheless been rubbing along together noticeably well in the Petrograd Soviet. Very much in the minority this time, the Bolsheviks there accepted the chairmanship of the Menshevik leader Nikolai Chkheidze. All this might have possibly altered very quickly if V. I. Lenin had got his way.

As the Communist author Andrew Rothstein admitted in his 1950 book, *Causes of the Russian Revolution*, there were strong reasons why the Bolsheviks were in a weak position to threaten the relative political order that reigned in the Russian capital in March 1917.

They at this stage had their organisation only in the larger factories: on them had fallen the brunt of the revolutionary illegal struggle against the war in the three preceding years, and hundreds of their active members were in exile. The Mensheviks and the Socialist-Revolutionaries, on the other hand, had had a semi-legal existence as supporters of the war. The Bolshevik delegates in the Soviet, therefore, were completely outnumbered by their opponents; and the Soviet majority endorsed the transformation of the Duma Leaders' Committee into a Provisional Government. The predominance of the Menshevik and Socialist-Revolutionaries in the Petrograd Soviet – and in other Soviets which began to spring up in town and country – seemed to guarantee that the workers and peasants whom they represented would in fact accept the modest role to which Menshevik theory assigned them.

With the Tsar safely imprisoned at his palace in Tsarskoe Selo a few miles south of Petrograd, digging up the lawns for vegetable gardens and sawing and stacking firewood, and the war against Germany and Austria–Hungary stalled because the Germans did not want to undertake any new offensives that might unify Russians, the Provisional Government had a brief breathing space in which to establish itself in the people's affections and sympathy.

Into that moment – that extraordinary pregnant pause in history – stepped Vladimir Ilich Ulyanov (known to history as V. I. Lenin) on 3 April, bearing his message of unremitting hostility towards the Provisional Government and the uncompromising demand that the Bolsheviks first take over the Petrograd Soviet and then as soon as possible afterwards the governance of Russia itself. The truce was about to be ripped up by a man who had spent more than a decade in exile since the failed 1905 Revolution, and who knew that time was no longer on the Bolsheviks' side.

There is plenty of evidence besides his *April Theses* to suggest that Lenin was firmly opposed to the policy of competitive co-operation that the Bolsheviks had hitherto adopted towards the other parties in the Petrograd Soviet. He had heard about the Revolution just as he was setting off for the library in Zurich, where he used to work after lunch. Comrade M. G. Bronski had arrived at his lodgings at 14 Spiegelgasse breathless with the news that the Tsar had been deposed. Lenin spent the rest of the day and night reading the newspapers pasted up beside Lake Geneva, telegraphing the Bolshevik Central Committee, and of course celebrating the downfall of the dynasty that had hanged his brother.

The telegrams that he sent – via his friend Alexandra Kollontai in Oslo, because the Russian secret police, the Okhrana, would intercept anything he sent direct – constitute the first piece of evidence of Lenin's attitude. These telegrams absolutely insisted that there was to be no 'patriotic' support of the imperialist war, no compromises (let alone alliances) with the Mensheviks, and that nothing must be done to aid the progressive programmes of the Provisional Government. All power in Russia must be transferred as soon as possible, by whatever means, to the Bolsheviks on the Petrograd Soviet. After briefly considering trying to fly back to Russia, and even more briefly thinking about taking a train disguised as a Swedish deaf-mute, Lenin realised that the only way to return to the capital – where he desperately needed to be, no time could be lost – was by doing a deal with the sole body (besides the Bolsheviks) who really wanted him to return there: the German Government.

Since it was in their interests to have as much political mayhem in the east as possible, the German authorities willingly laid on a special train service for thirty-one returning Russian émigrés. It left from the Swiss–German border at Schaffhausen on 27 March and took them all the way to the Stockholm ferry. Among the nineteen Bolsheviks on board were Grigori and Olga Safarov, Zinoviev, Radek and Lenin's former mistress Inessa Armand. There was no doubt who was in control, however, as was proven when Lenin – who was travelling with his wife Nadya Krupskaya – banned all smoking except in the lavatories, and then proceeded to issue tickets for their use. For each according to his needs . . .

The next piece of evidence that Lenin would accept no compromise with the Provisional Government came when, after crossing Sweden and Finland, the two editors of the

Bolshevik newspaper *Pravda*, Lev Kamenev and Joseph Stalin, boarded the train twenty miles north of Petrograd at Beloostrov. Back in Sweden and Finland, Lenin had read *Pravda*, which had called for pressure to be put on the Provisional Government to end the war, but also said that until that happened, the Russian soldier must 'firmly stand at his post, and answer bullet for bullet, shell for shell'. Without even greeting the comrades he had not seen for many years, Lenin launched into an immediate tirade: 'What have you been writing in *Pravda*? We've seen a few copies and have called you all sorts of names!'

Lenin was certain he was going to be arrested by the Provisional Government when he reached the Petrograd terminus called the Finland Station, and he even practised his courtroom defence speech. A Bolshevik women's delegation that boarded the train, including his younger sister Maria, nevertheless assured him that his reception was in fact going to be rapturous. And so it proved.

Soon after the lights of the train could be seen to the north, the chuntering of its twelve carriages could be heard as they slowed towards the station platform. As it pulled in, a few minutes after 11 p.m., its passengers could see a large welcoming committee from the Petrograd Soviet led by Chkheidze and comprising Mensheviks and Socialist-Revolutionaries, as well as Bolsheviks. There were also two companies of sailors in full-dress white uniform, mutineers from the Kronstadt garrison who were drawn up and presented arms under the command of their young Bolshevik officer. A huge bouquet of red roses was given to Lenin, as searchlights that had been taken from the Peter-Paul Fortress were trained on the returning hero. The crowds that had turned up, even at that time of night, numbered in their thousands. In the street outside there was an armoured car that had been laid on by the Bolshevik Central Committee, from the roof of which Comrade Lenin was slated to speak immediately after his official reception.

A non-Party socialist called Nikolai Sukhanov was present when Lenin first stepped onto Russian soil from his long years of exile, who recorded the scene in his book *Notes on Kerensky's Revolution*. His is the best eyewitness account for what happened next. There was a reception room at the station, ironically enough originally built for the Imperial family, and Sukhanov recalled Lenin striding into it at almost running pace as he came up to Chkheidze, who proceeded to make a speech. With that superb rudeness towards his political enemies that he had spent a lifetime perfecting, Lenin was 'looking as if all this that was happening only a few feet away did not concern him in the least; he glanced from one side to the other, looked the surrounding public over, and even examined the ceiling of the "Tsar's Room" while rearranging his bouquet (which harmonised rather badly with this whole figure)'.

When Chkheidze had finished, Lenin, ignoring him, turned away from the welcoming committee and addressed the crowd beyond them. 'Dear Comrades, soldiers, sailors and workers,' he began, and at that moment the bullet hit him just under the peak of his floppy cap, smashing straight through his forehead.

At first there was pandemonium, people flung themselves to the ground and the sailors quickly loaded their rifles, but once it became clear that no more shots were being fired, order was somehow regained. The assassin was wrestled to the ground by bystanders, then arrested by the police and hauled off to the Peter-Paul Fortress, where it was quickly ascertained that his name was Lev Harveivic Oswalt, an *odinokiy volk* (lone wolf) gunman with a Baltic patronymic, whose motive has never been satisfactorily established since he himself was murdered in police custody the very next day by a man with underworld connections. Aficionados of the mystery will be familiar with the various conspiracy theories – usually involving the Okhrana – on the subject of 'Who Shot V.I.L.?'.

Lenin's huge funeral was held two days later. The solemn procession began at the Bolsheviks' headquarters, the Kshessinskaya Palace (formerly the residence of the Tsar's first love, the prima ballerina Matilda Kshessinskaya). From the grandeur of its frescoed ceilings, bronze statues, wide staircase, huge gilt mirrors, crystal candelabra and satin upholstery, the coffin was taken to the Volkovoe Cemetery where Lenin was laid to rest beside his mother Maria and his sister Olga. The panegyrics were delivered by Kamenev and Zinoviev, who both chose to dwell on the past services Lenin had rendered the Party since its foundation in London in 1903, rather than his plans for its future. To Krupskaya's fury the *April Theses* were not only not published, but the Party ordained that they should be kept secret. They were only finally published as part of a Ph.D. thesis by a researcher from the University of Wisconsin in 1966, a full forty years after the Bolshevik Party had finally wound itself up.

For the bald fact was that apart from Krupskaya, Alexandra Kollontai and Alexander Shlyapnikov, virtually nobody in the senior ranks of the Bolshevik Party approved of Lenin's policy of total disengagement with the other parties and pursuit of the single goal of 'All power to the Soviets'. When Kollontai supported Shlyapnikov's attempt to promote Lenin's supposed programme in the Central Committee they were slapped down by the veteran Bolshevik Alexander Bogdanov with the words: 'You ought to be ashamed to applaud this nonsense – you cover yourselves with shame! And you call yourselves Marxists!'

Most Bolsheviks considered that the time had come to protect the revolutionary gains already made from the undoubted outside threats posed by international capitalism and also from the domestic threat represented by Tsarist and militarist reactionaries. The whole of the political Left must now coalesce, argued Zinoviev and Kamenev in their funeral orations, rather than fracture any further. This was certainly the line that *Pravda* continued to take on the orders of the

Central Committee, and it could claim a notable victory when in late April the Provisional Government announced Russia's withdrawal from the imperialist war.

With the incisive thinking that always characterised Prince Lvov's government, the decision was taken that since almost all of Russia's troubles essentially stemmed from the war, a peace treaty must be signed immediately at almost any price. Sure enough, the price that Berlin charged was horrifically high, but nonetheless Guchkov travelled to Brest-Litovsk to sign it on 27 April 1917. 'Of course the peace we shall conclude will be a foul peace,' he readily admitted to the Cabinet, 'but we need delay in order to give effect to social reforms ... it is essential for us to consolidate ourselves.' Nor were the combined protestations, pleadings and threats of David Lloyd George, Georges Clemenceau and Woodrow Wilson allowed to have any effect on the Provisional Government, which recognised that its survival depended on securing peace. Russia gave up many of the territories she had captured since the reign of Catherine the Great, including Western Latvia, Lithuania, Poland, most of Estonia, large parts of Ukraine, and Kars and Batum in the Caucasus. Finland became fully independent. Despite the grave loss to Russia in terms of coal and iron ore deposits, millions of population and thousands of engineering factories, the peace treaty was ratified by the Duma.

True to the Provisional Government's hopes and suspicions, the treaty was thankfully only short-lived. With America in the war against the Central Powers from April 1917, Germany's ultimate defeat was certain, despite the forces she was able to transfer from her eastern to her western front, and it finally came in March 1919. Although she was not invited to the Versailles peace conference, Russia was able by *force majeure* to cancel many of the provisions of Brest-Litovsk and retake all her lost provinces except Poland.

The anger with which the terms of Brest-Litovsk had been greeted in Petrograd soon subsided when millions of soldiers were able to return to their villages in time for the 1917 summer harvest. With peace and bread-supplies now delivered, the Lvov government turned its attentions to providing land and freedom for ordinary Russians. Soon the Bolsheviks found that their most popular slogan – 'Peace! Land! Bread!' – had been appropriated in every particular by a ministry whose principal force, Alexander Kerensky, was determined that no one could occupy the ground to the left of him. It was Kerensky who pushed through the far-reaching anti-corruption laws that significantly improved the hitherto sclerotic and inefficient Russian administrative government. He expropriated all Imperial and Church lands, and nationalised the estates of 150 of the largest Tsarist landowners in Russia, for the benefit of the local peasantry. All the old feudal laws were repealed and land expropriated from the peasantry at the time of the abolition of serfdom in 1861 was restored to them. The liberals in Lvov's government, including its President, went along with the thirty-six-year-old Kerensky, recognising that he was by far the lesser of the available political evils.

Kerensky appreciated the truth that Prince Louis-Napoleon had learned in France in the late 1840s, that if they were treated with honour and generosity, the richer peasants could become a deeply conservative force in society. Kerensky simultaneously pursued his left-wing agenda in the factories, where workers' councils were given legal parity with the industrialists, and those few lockouts that did occur were immediately broken by the police.

Since Lenin's assassination the Bolsheviks had found they had lost the initiative; for all the sympathy his funeral had evinced, their calls for open treaties, the cancellation of all debts and for workers' takeovers of all factories were widely seen as naïvely utopian. Furthermore their call for the 'liberation' of all of Russia's remaining colonies sounded deeply unpatriotic, especially after the humiliation of Brest-Litovsk. It was therefore politically possible for Kerensky to arrest the

Menshevik agitator Leon Trotsky as he returned to Russia from North America in May 1917, without a rupture either with the Petrograd Soviet or the leftist parties.

One decision that threatened to increase support for the Bolsheviks in August was that of allowing the Romanovs to go into exile, rather than their being put on trial for treason. The Foreign Minister and former monarchist Milyukov came under great pressure to resign after it was announced that the Imperial family had left for Switzerland, in a deal brokered by Lord Bertie, the British ambassador in Paris. 'I shall always remain your true and devoted friend as you know I have been in the past,' King George V had written to his cousin on 19 March, and of course he was utterly true to his word.

An arrangement was negotiated with the Austro-Hungarians by which the ex-Tsar and his family crossed the border by train and proceeded to the Swiss border, whence they settled in Gstaad. Over the next five decades the lives and loves of the Tsarevich and his four grand-duchess sisters were to fill the pages of the world's society columns, but the Romanov-Theodoracopulos family – as they were eventually to become – were never again to intrude onto the front pages, to their own considerable relief.

They owed their survival to Milyukov's diplomacy and to Kerensky's clemency. 'I will not be the Marat of the Russian Revolution,' the latter said, as the family left Tsarskoe Selo for the last time. 'The Russian Revolution does not take vengeance.' Although the Bolsheviks made some political capital out of the Romanovs' escape – Zinoviev famously denouncing the way that the royals had been 'transported in a sealed train like a plague bacillus' – the issue did not last long once the family were safely installed in Gstaad's Palace Hotel. (The jewels the grand-duchesses had prudently stitched into their dresses later allowed the Romanovs to buy the compound of hillside chalets that they occupy to this day.)

Instead, attention was occupied by the bewildering series

of radical reforms that Kerensky embarked upon, each designed to cut the political ground from under the Bolsheviks and Mensheviks. Instead of the Bolsheviks' plans for wholesale land nationalisation, Kerensky provided wide-ranging schemes of what he called 'land socialisation'. These gave power to agrarian councils, which soon proved popular with the *kulaks* (the better-off peasants), who tended to dominate them. Widely recognised as the protector of the working man against the big industrialists, bankers and landlords, Kerensky found himself capable of dealing with the gross dislocation of industry and commerce, and especially the transport problems, that had been caused by the war. His eight-hour-day legislation proved highly popular with workers. All imperialist designs against the Ottoman Empire were dropped, even once that entity imploded after its defeat at the hands of the Allies in 1918.

Not only did Kerensky not see himself as the Marat of the Russian Revolution, but he also refused to be its Bonaparte. Although Russia was unused to existence without an autocrat, it managed to learn the art of pluralist liberal democracy with surprising rapidity once it became clear than neither Kamenev's Bolsheviks nor General Kornilov's Tsarists had the depth of support among the masses to overthrow the status quo. The writer V. V. Shulgin described Kerensky as 'one of those who can dance on a marsh', and the Minister for Justice certainly lived up to the reputation. 'He spoke decisively, authoritatively,' wrote Shulgin, 'as one who has not lost his head ... He seemed to grow every minute.' Kerensky alone saved the life of the Tsarist minister Protopopov who was about to be lynched at the Tauride Palace in March 1917 with the command: 'Don't dare touch that man! The Duma does not shed blood.' He underlined this when he abolished capital punishment the following month. His nationalisation of large parts of the Russian banking system in December 1917 stole almost the last of the Bolsheviks' political clothes. (The banks were denationalised in the 1920s, it is true, but by then the issue no longer exercised the same sensitivity.)

The Bolsheviks' nakedness was made plain to all in the All-Russia general election of February 1918, which produced a Duma that few would have prophesied even so much as twelve months earlier. Kerensky's Socialist-Revolutionary Party made amazing strides against both Mensheviks and Bolsheviks – the latter of which vacillated between boycotting the elections and fighting them, with predictably disastrous results. Kerensky succeeded Prince Lvov as President, a post he was to hold on and off until his triumphant retirement in the wake of the Munich Victory twenty years later.

As the American journalist John Reed recorded in his book on the 1918 election campaign, *Ten Days That Shook the Bolsheviks*, the results were so disastrous for Lenin's former party that many forsook it altogether. Zinoviev wound up as a successful scriptwriter in 1920s Hollywood; Stalin made a great success of running a chain of abattoirs back in the Caucasus, and when Trotsky was finally released from the Peter-Paul Fortress he found that neither the Mensheviks themselves nor the Bolsheviks he had opposed for years were interested in his revolutionary Leninist theories. Few, however, would have predicted his ultimate fate as a mountaineering accessories salesman in Mexico.

That the Kerensky governments drew back during the 1920s and 1930s from many of their more left-wing positions was only to be expected. Russia's strengths in raw materials and tertiary education and her enormous domestic consumption capacity meant that she weathered the Great Depression better than many other European countries, including her old enemy Germany. In the 1940s Russia enjoyed a hugely prosperous economic boom which many Russians rightly today see as that country's golden age.

Yet nothing in history is inevitable; if Oswalt had fired a few inches to the right or left of V. I. Lenin's head that fateful night in early April 1917, it is perfectly possible to believe that the Bolsheviks might have adopted the radical course of disengagement and revolutionary ardour that their comrade had already mapped out for them. Had Lenin been present to drag the Party constantly towards the most extreme course, to agitate ceaselessly against the Provisional Government throughout the spring and summer of 1917, it is not inconceivable – especially if the Lvov government had not made peace with Germany – that he might have engineered the conditions necessary for a *second* Russian revolution some time in the autumn of 1917.

Who is to say how Kerensky's political future might have fared if he had decided to continue fighting the war? Instead of being fêted as the father of the modern nation, as Washington, Gandhi and Atatürk are in their countries, he might have ended up as, say, a professor at Princeton, fated to be the punchline of modern history's saddest joke. Of course, counterfactuals lead on to further counterfactuals; there is no saying what kind of Soviet leader 'the dictatorship of the proletariat' might have thrown up by 1938, at the time of Adolf Hitler's Munich débâcle. When liberal-democratic Russia joined Neville Chamberlain's Anglo-French Coalition to stand up for the rights of Czechoslovakia that year – along with Denmark, Poland, Holland and Romania – it of course led to the overthrow of the Nazi regime that year. A Bolshevik regime might not have proved such an attractive ally for the West; of such things we can never know.

The only memorial to V. I. Lenin today is a small marble bust in the Volkovoe Cemetery in Petrograd, giving his name and dates – baldly stating 'V. I. Ulyanov (known as "Lenin") 1870–1917' – and underneath a quotation from a lecture he gave on 22 January 1917, only ten weeks before his death, to some students in Zurich, in which he uncannily prophesied: 'We of the older generation may not live to see the decisive battles of this coming Revolution.'

Memorials to Alexander Kerensky, of course, are numbered in their hundreds all across the Russian Union; statues, parks, libraries, the Kerensky Prospekt in Moscow and the city of Kerenskigrad (formerly Volgagrad) among them. Such are the rewards of great statesmanship.

Stalin Flees Moscow in 1941

Simon Sebag Montefiore

At 4 a.m. on the morning of Friday 17 October 1941, a tiny figure in boots, an old First World War greatcoat with darned pockets, a fur *shapka* hat with earmuffs and a slightly stiff left arm stood alone on the ill-lit platform of a timber-storage siding on the Moscow outskirts amidst the steam that billowed from the engine of an armoured train. The glint of the tommy-guns of his bodyguards could be seen at either end of the platform. A table had been set up in the midst of the platform bearing a line of telephones. There was nothing else besides the boom of distant howitzers.

The sturdy little man, haggard-faced, yellow-eyed, scrawny-necked, was quite alone and utterly still, sometimes almost disappearing into the steam. Then the train driver shovelled another load of coal into the engine. The train seemed to shiver and a thick jet of steam burst into the freezing October air completely enveloping the small figure on the platform. The guards leant forward, narrowing their eyes to see if he was still there. After all, their fates – indeed the destiny of Russia and the whole world at war – seemed to depend on his decision.

Almost twenty-four hours earlier, at 8 a.m. on 16 October, Joseph Vissarionovich Stalin, Premier of the Soviet Government (Chairman of the Council of People's Commissars) and General Secretary of the Bolshevik Party, Lenin's successor, had summoned the Politburo to the Kremlin for what was probably the most sensational meeting of his entire career. There was now no doubt that Operation Typhoon, Adolf Hitler's final push to take Moscow, had broken through. Just under two weeks earlier, on 3 October, General Heinz

Guderian's Panzers had smashed a gaping hole in the Russian front line to the south, taking the city of Orel, 125 miles behind the supposed front.

The following day Stalin had lost contact with General Ivan Koniev's Western Front. The Briansk and Reserve Fronts were shattered, leaving a twelve-mile gap in the defences of Moscow. Then, on the 5th, the Moscow air force commander Sbytov had reported that a column of German tanks were heading up the Ukhnovo highway straight towards Moscow. While Stalin's secret police chief and fellow-Georgian, Lavrenti Beria, threatened the air force with charges of treason, Stalin realised the reports were true: 'Act decisively and energetically,' he ordered. 'Mobilise every available resource to hold the enemy.' Stalin telephoned his best and most ruthless commander, General Georgi Zhukov, who had just successfully saved the besieged city of Leningrad, and ordered him to fly down to take control of Moscow's frayed defences. Rushing to Stalin's apartment in the Kremlin, Zhukov found an exhausted leader, suffering from influenza, telling Beria to sound out the possibilities of making peace with Hitler. Stalin then dispatched Zhukov straight to the Western Front. There, in the chaos of retreat and recrimination, Zhukov took Koniev as his deputy and started work. 'If Moscow falls,' Stalin told them, 'both your heads will roll.'

As Zhukov fought for time, the struggle reached a frenzy of steel and snow, flesh and dynamite, mud and mayhem. The towns of Kalinin to the north and Kaluga to the south of Moscow both fell. Panzer tanks motored across the battlefield of Borodino. In Moscow, the panic spread from the Kremlin to the streets. Law and order collapsed. By 14 October, food shops were being looted, apartments burgled, refugees blocked the streets, smoke from bonfires darkened the skies, while gangs of desperadoes, thieves and deserters terrorised the Muscovites. At the railway stations there were riots as the families of grandees jostled with those of ordinary citizens to catch the trains to safety in the east.

The panic came straight from the top: Stalin's grandees, those powerful Politburo magnates and People's Commissars, Beria, Lazar Kaganovich and Georgi Malenkov felt the regime was tottering. 'We shall be shot like partridges,' Beria told them. These Soviet potentates advised Stalin to evacuate Moscow. Stalin revealed nothing, presenting an air of inscrutable solitude to his lieutenants. In the Kremlin, his officials were shocked to see that he was now as thin 'as a bag of bones' with his tunics hanging off him. He was reading the histories of Marshal Prince Kutuzov and his abandonment of Moscow to Napoleon in 1812; on his own copy he scrawled, 'We shall overcome.' But there were other moments when his nerves seemed close to breaking point; he grumbled to one general that his phone never stopped ringing with reports of 'German parachutists' landing in the middle of Moscow. At one point he called General Koniev, sounding almost deranged. 'Comrade Stalin's not a traitor. Comrade Stalin's an honourable man,' he said, speaking of himself in the third person. Stalin's staff prepared for his escape; his library was loaded into his private armoured train. Four American Douglas DC-3 airplanes stood at the ready. By the 16th, when he drove at dawn into the Kremlin, he passed looting mobs in the streets. At 9 a.m. the leadership met in Stalin's apartment. Stalin ordered the evacuation to the ancient city of Samara on the Volga, which had been renamed Kuibyshev since 1935 after the late Politburo member, Valerian Kuibyshev.

Vyacheslav Molotov, former Premier and now Foreign Commissar, and Anastas Mikoyan, his two most efficient and trusted Old Bolshevik workhorses, were to superintend the evacuation, while Kaganovich was to provide the trains. Stalin suggested that the Politburo leave that day: 'I will leave tomorrow morning,' he added. Outside in the city, workers at the factories were no longer being paid. Demolition squads dynamited the Metro and the bridges across the Moskva. Officials simply abandoned their posts. Even the British embassy right opposite the Kremlin was abandoned by its guards and looted. Molotov and Mikoyan supervised the evacuation of foreign diplomats and the Soviet government to Kuibyshev. Yet would Stalin really abandon Moscow? Would the USSR crumble if he left the city? Would it mean the end of the Stalinist-Leninist empire and the start of Hitler's Thousand-Year Reich? Would Britain stand alone – or would Churchill be forced to seek peace? If Moscow fell, would Japan change her plans to attack the American naval base at Pearl Harbor and invade Russia instead? Everything hung on Stalin's decision.

All day he seemed to probe his comrades and staff but no one knew his thoughts. Leaving his Kremlin apartment, Stalin temporarily disappears from history for a few hours. But amongst his trusted bodyguards was a suave Georgian named Colonel Tengiz Fiktionashvili, who was trusted by Stalin because he came from near the dictator's own home town of Gori and was not one of Beria's Mingrelian cronies. Before his own execution, Fiktionashvili wrote an account of these days which this author discovered forgotten and mislaid in a file marked 'Evidence of L. P. Beria's Treatment for VD' and which are revealed here for the first time.

Guarded now by the omnipresent Fiktionashvili, who witnessed all the events of the following days, Stalin moved down into his plywood headquarters deep underground in the marble tunnels of the Kirov Metro station and continued working ... Molotov, Mikoyan, Beria and the others arrived for a late dinner, exhausted by the vast enterprise of evacuating the capital. Over dinner, Beria urged Stalin to leave while there was still time.

'Joseph Vissarionovich,' he said, 'You are too important to risk yourself in the ruins of Moscow!' Then he switched to Georgian: 'It's just a city! Just bricks and mortar! Let them take it!'

'Speak Russian if you have anything to say,' retorted Stalin.

Molotov and the others watched him closely but he gave

away nothing. Then, at about 1 a.m., Stalin's direct line rang and he took the call.

'I'm listening,' he snapped as usual.

Molotov and Beria guessed it was Zhukov from the front.

'Can you hold Moscow? Tell me as a Bolshevik?'

He listened, put down the phone and sighed. 'Zhukov's front is crumbling but he thinks he can hold them on a new line. It's going to cost us! We really fucked it up. Vecha!' He turned to Molotov. 'Have you read the story of 1812?' He gruffly tossed Molotov his copy of Kutuzov's biography then smiled grimly: 'Obligatory reading!'

Molotov and Beria exchanged looks; they remembered Stalin's breakdown after the first week of the war when Hitler took Minsk. Then Stalin had said, 'Lenin left us a state and we've fucked it up' before retiring to his dacha in a state of listless depression. He expected to be arrested but they had summoned him back to supreme command as chairman of a new State Defence Committee and forgiven his mistakes; after all, he had slaughtered any opposition in the Great Terror of 1937 and they knew no other way but Stalin's way. Nonetheless, they had seen then a glimmer of weakness in his steely armour and none could forget it.

Just before 4 a.m., Stalin called General Nikolai Vlasik, his burly and trusted Chief of Security, and Alexander Poskrebyshev, his hideous *chef de cabinet*, as well as Fiktionashvili, and ordered them to accompany him. Only when he was climbing into his car did he instruct the driver to take them to the Abelmanovsky railway siding where his train waited. With their hearts beating they watched him walking heavily up and down the platform. When the steam from the locomotive cleared, Stalin was gone.

Vlasik and Poskrebyshev ordered the guards to mount the train and clambered aboard themselves. Fiktionashvili cast one more glance over Moscow and followed them. They found Stalin in his special carriage that he had 'borrowed' from a museum: it had once belonged to Tsar Nicholas II. 'Your orders, Comrade Stalin?' asked Vlasik, standing to attention. 'To Kuibyshev!' replied Stalin, his face a mask. Fiktionashvili hurried out and the train shook and then gathered speed. When the Georgian returned, Stalin smiled at him: 'Don't worry, boy,' he said. 'They'll choke on Moscow.' Within seconds, one of the security officers on the now-abandoned platform was calling his boss, Beria, on the phones on that table. He jabbered excitedly in Georgian. Beria replaced the phone in his bunker beneath the Lubianka Prison, gave the orders to his NKVD Special Tasks teams to put his resistance plan into motion – and called Molotov on the *vertushka* special Kremlin phone: 'He's gone. Will you join me in my Douglas?' Molotov, who had grabbed some sleep in his office in the Kremlin air-raid shelter, called Mikoyan and then Kaganovich and so on. All of them warned their friends and ordered their guards to summon their Packard limousines to take them to Kazan Station or their special airfields. Within minutes the word had spread: the Politburo was fleeing. Almost immediately, the last fetters of Stalinist discipline were broken. Thousands of people were trampled underfoot at the stations; fires started in apartment buildings; the last shops were looted; secret policemen and soldiers tore off their uniforms and ran; the whole city was on the move, trying to head east in cars, trucks, tanks, on donkeys and even horse-drawn carts. Yet within the armed forces itself and the NKVD divisions placed around Moscow, it was different. Within seconds of Stalin's train pulling away, General Zhukov was called by one of his ADCs at the headquarters in Moscow and told that 'The *Khozyain* [Master] has left the city'. Zhukov knew that his own head was on the line but he understood too that Moscow should not now be defended. If the Wehrmacht occupied Moscow, it would be only insecurely and for a short time. It would be their graveyard. But it was up to Zhukov to take that dread decision and face the contempt of posterity for abandoning Holy Moscow.

Zhukov believed that he could have held the city had Stalin remained – his very name and presence were enough to stiffen resistance. But now he had gone and there was a danger that Zhukov's armies could disintegrate. Yet abandoning Moscow, as they had abandoned Kiev, made military sense. Zhukov would dig in around the vast factories of the eastern suburbs and suck the over-confident Germans into deadly street-fighting, fortify the line behind Moscow between Kolomna and Noginsk and then counter-attack with the fresh reserves arriving from the Far East. Faced with a renewed push by the Germans and the possibility of being surrounded by the Panzer pincers in Moscow, Zhukov ordered an orderly retreat and left Moscow to its terrible fate.

Beria's NKVD shadowed every military division as the withdrawal took place; there were few desertions. Any lack of discipline meant instant execution. But the sight of vast bodies of troops, tanks and trucks rushing eastwards through Moscow only redoubled the chaos and fear in the streets. Meanwhile Stalin's train headed through the darkness towards his new capital, Kuibyshev, where he would gather the Politburo. He was determined to lead the Soviet Union to victory and he had no doubt in his mind that he would imminently use his reserves to defeat the Germans in a battle of Moscow, hold them in the south and then lead his forces all the way to Berlin, like the Empress Elisabeth and Emperor Alexander I before him. The sacrifices, as his abandonment of Moscow proved, were great but Kutuzov, who had abandoncd the city in 1812, was still a peerless hero. Besides, if necessary Zhukov and Koniev would take the blame. Their heads would roll . . .

Just hours later, German advance units found the Kremlin undefended and hoisted the Swastika from its towers, ripping down the red and gold stars with which Stalin had recently embellished them. Beria's plans for a street-by-street sabotage of the German advance did not materialise and the centre fell swiftly and easily into German hands. At the Wolf's Lair headquarters in East Prussia, Adolf Hitler immediately insisted on visiting the Kremlin – even though there was still fighting in Moscow's eastern suburbs and the city itself was hardly secure. His lightning two-hour visit at dawn on 1 November, accompanied by Göring, Himmler and his entourage, was a characteristic *coup de théâtre* – a mixture of triumphalism, sightseeing and propaganda. The Führer toured the Kremlin, visited Stalin's apartments and admired Ivan the Terrible's tomb in the Archangel Cathedral. He then led Reichsmarschall Göring and Joseph Goebbels up the steps to the Lenin Mausoleum, where they were photographed laughing – a picture that was beamed across the world. (Stalin had sent Lenin's mummy to the east at the start of the war.)

The news arrived that a General Vlasov and a group of senior Soviet officers had defected and offered to lead a Russian national army against Stalin. Although some Nazi leaders suggested that such an army would exploit Russian nationalism and accelerate the fall of the Soviet regime, Heinrich Himmler retorted that Slavs could never bear arms in the Third Reich and Hitler backed him. 'Their defection and warm welcome must be filmed and announced,' he commanded, 'but in reality our brutality towards the Slavs must be a legend for evermore like that of Tamerlane.' Meanwhile, Goebbels cleverly ordered that the first copy of the film of the Führer's visit to the Lenin Mausoleum be dropped by parachute onto Stalin's headquarters in Kuibyshev. We now know from Colonel Fiktionashvili's papers that it changed history.

The Politburo watched the film together. The sight of Hitler at the Kremlin chilled them. There was silence afterwards as they felt Stalin's invincibility diminished as Hitler strutted on the Mausoleum, their Holy of Holies. Silence was the only way the Politburo expressed its disapproval in those years of fear. Stalin said nothing but stood up and walked out: 'We've fucked up!' he muttered, casting a yellow stare at Beria: 'So much for your special operations to make every street in the centre of Moscow a battlefield ... there are clearly traitors in your departments. You screwed up, Beria.' He paused: 'I resign and hand over to the Central Committee.' He retired to his villa by the Volga to calm himself. While he was there, his daughter Svetlana, who had been sent back to Kuibyshev earlier in the war, called on him and remembered that 'he had never been more weary and downcast'.

The Politburo continued its meeting. First there was silence but then Deputy Premier Nikolai Voznesensky, the brash, handsome young economist from Leningrad who was close to Molotov, asked:

'What do we do now?' He then turned to Molotov and asked him: 'We need you, Vecha: please lead us.'

'Comrade Stalin is our leader,' retorted Molotov.

'Comrade Stalin is our leader,' repeated Beria shrewdly, 'but are we not obliged to follow his own order to summon the Central Committee?'

'To discuss the decision to abandon Moscow,' added Voznesensky, who alone dared to say the unsayable.

Beria understood that he would probably be executed for the failures of his operations. He had nothing to lose. Afterwards, Beria and General Zhukov secretly conferred and it was agreed that the army and even the security forces had certain questions that could only be asked at a Central Committee meeting. 'We certainly did not have to withdraw from Moscow. That was panic plain and simple,' said Zhukov bluntly. He would not normally have trusted Beria, but since he knew he would otherwise bear the blame for Moscow he too felt he had little to lose. Besides, he was seething at Stalin's bungling. By chance, even Molotov and Kaganovich believed it was now necessary to call such a session, but they were not included in Beria's talks with the army for fear that they would run straight to Stalin.

The members of the Central Committee had been elected

at the 18th Congress in 1939, and were thus the new generation of Stalinists who had risen over the bodies of those killed in the Terror. It was hard to imagine a more cowed and emasculated organ. The State Defence Committee summoned those of its members who had managed to make it to Kuibyshev. Stalin himself remained closeted at his villa and it was assumed he was suffering another breakdown. When the Central Committee met the following day, Stalin was invited to attend but did not appear for its opening at 9 a.m.

In classic Bolshevik style, the Plenum – for we now have the secret stenographic records of Politburo and CC sessions – began with Molotov praising Stalin's leadership, the decision to abandon Moscow and asking for a vote of confidence in him. Voznesensky next stood up: 'I too praise Comrade Stalin's leadership but I believe, comrades, that we must all share the blame for some of the decisions that were taken.' Beria, Khrushchev and other young leaders also gradually watered down Molotov's original statement until it merely praised Stalin's 'outstanding and brilliant' leadership during industrialisation, collectivisation and the struggle against Trotskyites, but merely mentioned his 'firm' leadership during the war. Even this vote was received with a marked lack of enthusiasm.

It was then that Voznesensky asked General Zhukov whether he believed that the abandonment of Moscow had been 'necessary'.

'It was one of the alternatives,' he replied. 'I completely supported the wisdom of Comrade Stalin.'

But it was Beria who amazed the gathering by pressing the point:

'Did you not just tell me, Comrade Zhukov, that you could have held Moscow but abandoned it because of the panic on high?'

This was classic Beria, for had Stalin returned to power he could have claimed credit for exposing the general's treason. But the words had been said; various other speakers now called tentatively for Stalin to be summoned. The State Defence Committee was assigned to request his attendance. Stalin had weathered such storms before, but when the State Defence Committee found him in the library at his villa, he did not even look up. Only when Molotov pulled up a chair beside him and beseeched him to come did he rise to his feet and accompany them. When Voznesensky dutifully proposed Stalin's re-election to the General Secretaryship of the Party, Stalin merely said quietly: 'I am at the disposal of the CC' – and stalked out. Depressed and broken, he hardly seemed capable of defending himself.

Yet on returning to his villa, Stalin summoned Beria and ordered him to arrest all those in the State Defence Committee spreading 'slander and defeatism such as Molotov. They must be executed.' Beria sycophantically agreed but instead rushed to tell Molotov and the others. They were terrified of Stalin's vengeance. Gradually, darting purposefully from leader to leader, Beria won their support to arrest Stalin and appoint Molotov as General Secretary. Known as a rigid plodder, a stickler for detail, nicknamed Iron Arse by Lenin, who denounced his 'idiotic bureaucraticism', Molotov was nonetheless the only candidate with the prestige to do the job.

Molotov had already served as Premier from 1930–1940 and Lenin himself had appointed him as Secretary of the Party in 1921, so officially he had preceded Stalin in both jobs. Molotov had long been the second man of the regime: whcn IIitler had invaded, il had been he rather than Stalin who had spoken to the Soviet people. Furthermore, the other candidates were inappropriate: Voroshilov was old and famously stupid; Mikoyan and Kaganovich were not Russian (being Armenian and Jewish); Andrei Zhdanov was besieged in Leningrad; while of the younger generation, Beria (also not a Russian), Voznesensky and Ukrainian boss Nikita Khrushchev were too new to the top table.

Beria briefed only his own fellow Mingrels to arrest Stalin

and then called the villa. There was no time to waste; Stalin was close to his guards and many of the secret policemen – but, as agreed, Colonel Fiktionashvili answered the phone. He knew what to do. He pushed open the door of the little library where Stalin was sitting rereading an old story by Chekhov that he had always loved. He did not even look up when the NKVD Colonel drew his Nagan pistol just as Beria's convoy of Buick cars screeched to a halt outside the house. Stalin had not known that Fiktionashvili had been arrested in the twenties for murdering a family and raping the women; Beria had saved and promoted him. He owed everything to Beria.

'I'm not surprised,' Stalin told Fiktionashvili. 'Ever since they killed Kirov, I've been wondering which of you will put a bullet into me – into my face or my back. I trusted no one. Not even myself. Sometimes I'm afraid of my own shadow . . .'

'I am sorry Joseph Vissarionovich,' replied Fiktionashvili, removing Stalin's own Mauser pistol from the pocket of his greatcoat, draped over a chair.

Beria, Rapava and Tsanava breathlessly entered the little library, Mausers drawn. Stalin greeted Beria in Georgian with a tone of relief but also a slightly Jesus-like disdain for his betrayer:

'You, Lavrenti Pavlovich? You who cared for my mother and was like a son to me? You?' Then he smiled thinly.

Stalin was held in the basement of the Party building, guarded by Beria and his Mingrelians. When the State Defence Committee met upstairs, Stalin became a victim of his own system of life and death. The leaders, many such as Molotov and Mikoyan his close friends for almost thirty years of obscurity and power, had little faith that the master manipulator would remain for long in his cell. They knew only too well what he was capable of – and they feared his will, intelligence and subtlety. For the sake of the war, for their own survival, and according to the rules of Stalin's own system, he must now be tried. There was no time to spare, especially since Zhukov was urgently needed back at the front.

Ulrich, the bullet-headed Baltic bully who had sentenced so many innocent men to death at Stalin's bidding, chaired the secret sitting of his Military Collegium court that afternoon. In a shabby basement hall, while Beria and the others watched through a newly made hole in the damp wall, Stalin was accused of treason and defeatism in the abandonment of Moscow and duly sentenced to death.

'Have you anything to say, Comrade? I mean Prisoner Stalin?' Ulrich asked him, his voice quivering.

Stalin sighed and then said: 'I have devoted my life to Lenin and the Bolshevik Party and I will die as a devout knight of the proletariat. But I do appeal for mercy. I accept my own mistakes in retreating from Moscow but the city will soon be retaken. Its fall has broken the force of the Germans. The Far Eastern armies are now ready. If I have made mistakes, I accept them. I will die with Lenin's name on my lips,' he repeated quietly. 'I die as a Bolshevik.'

Stalin then contemptuously cast his yellow eyes over the gap in the wall through which the Politburo watched with ghastly fascination and strangely mixed emotions. For they were destroying their master, their father, their hero. The Politburo confirmed the court's sentence; Molotov and Voroshilov wept openly. Only Mikoyan abstained and only Kaganovich, Stalin's truest devotee, voted against. Khrushchev sobbed. The younger leaders, including Beria and Voznesensky who were only candidate Politburo members, were the most determined, but even Beria seemed deeply moved: 'Must I kill my own father for the Party?' Nonetheless he was resolute and, taking the signed scrap of paper, he hurried out.

Beria himself brought the NKVD's chief executioner, Blokhin, to perform the execution. With his thick hair and broad Tartar features, Blokhin had shot Zinoviev, Kamenev, Bukharin and many of Stalin's famous victims of the Terror.

He had donned a leather butcher's apron and cap so as not to spatter his NKVD uniform in the execution of thousands of Poles in the Katyn Forest massacre. Now, while Fiktionashvili kept guard outside, Beria, Blokhin and two of his fellow executioner-thugs from the Kommandatura department of the NKVD entered Stalin's cell.

Stalin was reading a biography of Ivan the Terrible, wearing his usual semi-military tunic and boots. He sat up when they entered:

'Well?'

'Comrade Stalin,' Beria began. 'Joseph Vissarionovich, the Politburo has upheld the sentence of the Military Collegium.'

Stalin stood up stiffly, wearily but with dignity; he was still the great world-historical man – but as he realised he was about to die, his legs gave way. The two secret policemen grabbed his arms while Beria and Blokhin watched in amazement.

'I always thought that Ivan the Terrible was poisoned,' mused Stalin.

Inside him, the grandeur of the man of steel wrestled with the fear of the human being. Stalin had always taken a special interest in the conduct of his victims as they were executed. Now he himself sobbed, then got hiccups and then started to shout Georgian insults so loudly that Beria stuffed a towel in his mouth, noticing that his trousers were now wet. Beria had seen many men die. Stalin was made to kneel facing the wall.

'Comrade Blokhin, perform the sentence of the Central Committee and Soviet government,' ordered Beria.

Blokhin stepped forward and drew his beloved Walther pistol. He levelled it at the back of Stalin's neck, that famous neck, grown thin from the stress of defeat, and fired. Everyone in the room froze with a sort of awe mixed with relief and regret.

Beria wiped his eyes; this man after all had found him and promoted him, spoiled him with privileges and brought him to Moscow to be a great man. But he had also terrorised him, humiliated him, turned him into a torturer. He had almost lost the war for Soviet Russia. He was a brute. Beria gathered himself and ordered Blokhin:

'Put the body into the drums of acid next door. No trace must survive or I'll rip your guts out.' Then he left. 'The fucker's gone,' he said to Fiktionashvili. 'Not a word or I'll grind you to campdust.'

As he hurried upstairs to the State Defence Committee, his hands were still shaking.

'Stalin is dead and gone,' he announced to the leaders. 'Now it is up to us. Comrade Molotov?'

Molotov's small stalwart frame, his almost square head, his bulging brow were all shaking and he was unable to speak. Voroshilov joined him in a chorus of childish weeping.

'Comrade Molotov, pull yourself together,' snapped Mikoyan.

Molotov stopped, pulled out a handkerchief and wiped his eyes like the good bourgeois that he had once been. Then he replaced his pince-nez and declared in a voice of surprisingly cold hardness, with even his lisp adding to the impression of determination:

'We will win the war. Of that there is no doubt. Marx always insisted it was not individuals that triumphed but the march of history. General Zhukov has told me that, as we expected, the German advance has played itself out. Their strength is being depleted in the fighting for the eastern suburbs of Moscow. Leningrad is holding and will not fall. By the sixth of December a counter-attack will retake Moscow, surround large forces there, and will throw back the Hitlerite invaders.'

And so it happened. When Zhukov attacked, using 400,000 fresh troops from the Far East with 1,000 new T-34 tanks and 1,000 new planes, many German units were surrounded in Moscow and the rest were thrown back 150 miles. Only then was it announced in a communiqué, signed by the

USSR's most celebrated doctors, that 'on 1 November, the heart of the beloved Soviet leader, Premier of the Soviet Government and General Secretary of the Bolshevik Party, J. V. Stalin, ceased to beat after suffering a colossal cerebral haemorrhage exacerbated by a history of various ailments including arterio-sclerosis, arthritis, and haemorrhoids'.

The Central Committee announced that Molotov had served as First Secretary and Premier since that date – with heroic consequences. The three executioners of Stalin were shot the next day, though Fiktionashvili was promoted. Stalin's 'ashes' were buried in the Kremlin wall, where they still rest in a position that seems appropriate to his ambiguous rank amongst Soviet leaders. The rumour naturally spread that he had suffered a stroke after the Central Committee Plenum where he was criticised and that Beria had hastened his death with poison.

Today Stalin is regarded by historians as a relatively minor figure in the Soviet pantheon compared to giants such as Lenin or Molotov. It is generally agreed that his Georgian background meant that he could never have roused Russian national spirit during the Great Patriotic War in the way that the ethnic Russian Molotov was able to do. Historians tend to believe that his military and diplomatic bungling would almost certainly have lost the USSR the war and that Beria's coup was most fortunate. Molotov remains one of the most enigmatic and fascinating historical titans, the subject of thousands of biographies and the true victor of the Second World War. It was Molotov who retook Moscow and, after some costly mistakes in 1942, presided over the decisive battle of Stalingrad. Molotov was able to learn from his generals such as Zhukov in a way that Stalin never could have. At the Tehran Conference and afterwards, Molotov impressed and charmed Churchill and Roosevelt with his quiet power, extraordinary abilities and urbane diplomatic finesse. The Grand Alliance broke down after the war just as Molotov secured a new Russian empire covering most of

Eastern Europe. When Truman announced that America possessed the atom bomb, Molotov placed Beria in charge and achieved parity in 1949.

Against his better judgement, Molotov was persuaded to accept the rank of Marshal and, after the war, that of Generalissimo – though his wife Polina told him that he looked absurd in a military uniform. After 1945, he stuck to his traditional suit and homburg hat. Jealous of Marshal Zhukov's glory and fame, he attacked him for 'self-promotion and Bonapartism' and demoted him in 1946. Molotov then reimposed discipline on his shattered land with a return to terror in the late forties and early fifties. He nominated Voznesensky, who had helped him to power, as his successor but then arrested and shot him in 1949 in the Leningrad Case.

Riots and unrest in East Berlin and some Soviet cities forced Molotov slightly to ease the repression after 1953, when he realised that Beria wished to liberalise the USSR and unite under his aegis the security organs. It was then that Molotov, aided by his Politburo colleagues Khrushchev, Malenkov, Bulganin and Marshal Zhukov, arrested Beria, who was tried and shot. (General Fiktionashvili, whose account has finally revealed the true fate of Stalin, was also executed with his master.) Beria was henceforth blamed for many of Molotov's own mistakes and repressions, joining Trotsky as the regime's chief villain. Molotov subsequently announced that Khrushchev was his ideal successor (though privately he regarded him as 'an ignorant bumpkin with no knowledge of Marxist texts'). At the 20th Congress in 1956 Molotov shocked the Soviet world by denouncing the brutality of the regime, blaming it on Stalin and Beria. When his heir apparent, Khrushchev, tried to defend the old ways and overthrow Molotov, he was outvoted and sent into internal exile to run a turnip farm. Marshal Zhukov backed Molotov again, was rewarded with the Ministry of Defence but was then dismissed again for 'Bonapartism'. Mikoyan,

Kaganovich and Malenkov survived as Molotov's junior partners in the Politburo and never challenged his supremacy.

Molotov, ever the diplomatic master, continued the relationship he had developed during the war with Eisenhower, with whom he worked to prevent a nuclear war. He thought Kennedy a 'likeable if weak spoilt boy with tendencies towards promiscuity' and LBJ a 'blustering blowhard primitive'. Shocked by JFK's assassination, he attended his funeral himself. Molotov remained a fanatical Marxist-Leninist but he built up his closest partnership with Richard Nixon and Dr Henry Kissinger, who shared his pragmatism in world affairs. Molotov loathed the 'crude peasant' Mao Tse-tung, 'that margarine Marxist', and thus proved unable to avoid the Sino-Soviet schism.

By 1960 Molotov, now aged seventy, was an absolute dictator dedicated to expanding Marxism while avoiding nuclear war with the West. But despite easing the old repression, he proved unable to stop Soviet stagnation. His invasion of Afghanistan in 1979 only highlighted Soviet weakness. By then, Molotov and his ageing comrade Kaganovich were respectively eighty-nine and eighty-six – Mikoyan had died in 1978 – but they showed no signs of retiring, and the new generation of leaders such as Leonid Brezhnev and Yuri Andropov were hardly much younger. Molotov's strong and intelligent Jewish wife Polina remained hugely powerful and super-elegant – now dressed by Yves Saint Laurent himself – and ever more unpopular when she was appointed Minister of Light Industry in 1956 and a member of the Politburo in 1964. Molotov never truly recovered from her death in 1970.

Molotov's chosen successors had been at various times the ebullient peasant Khrushchev, the bluff Brezhnev, the talented Andropov and the limited Chernenko – yet he outlived them all. His death in 1986, aged ninety-six, brought to power a new generation, led by Mikhail Gorbachev, who oversaw the collapse of the USSR, the retreat from Eastern Europe, the smashing of the Berlin Wall, the reunification of

Germany, the end of Russian communism, and the rise of gangster capitalism. Lying mummified beside Lenin, Molotov – this cruel, brutal, ruthless, rigid yet pragmatic Marxist bourgeois – remains the dominant statesman and monster of twentieth-century Russia.

The Japanese Do Not Attack Pearl Harbor

Conrad Black

As his isolationist opponents continuously alleged and Hitler feared, Franklin D. Roosevelt was determined to bring the United States into the European war eventually. Even without the Japanese attack and the subsequent German and Italian declarations of war on America, Roosevelt would have done so, admittedly by a more tortuous route and on an extended timescale. He was unshakeably determined to destroy Nazism and ultimately possessed the means to do so, albeit with allies, but allies substantially dependent on him.

Roosevelt well understood the strategic implications of the early actions of the Second World War in Europe. He had visited Europe in virtually every one of his first twenty-five years. His first schooling had been in Germany and he attended a full *Ring* cycle at Bayreuth in 1896, which he enjoyed but which fuelled his concerns about German militarism. He was the only American president in history who spoke both French and German. He had been a war hawk in World War I, when Assistant Secretary of the Navy, wanting an early US entry into the war on the side of the Allies. He even conspired with his cousin, Theodore Roosevelt, against the pacifist policy of his own president, Woodrow Wilson. Furthermore, he had been a student of the great naval strategist and historian Alfred Thayer Mahan, and had corresponded with Mahan when in Wilson's Navy Department.

There can be no doubt that Roosevelt realised from early in the 1930s that it might come to war with Germany. He told the French ambassador, Paul Claudel, at the beginning of his administration in 1933 that Hitler was a 'madman' and so were his principal henchmen in the new German government. In 1936, Roosevelt wrote to his cousin when Hitler reoccupied the Rhineland to say that France had to occupy Germany up to the Rhône at once, for within a year Germany would be stronger than France and a rearmed Germany would break the peace. Roosevelt had abandoned hope for peaceful relations with Hitler even before Winston Churchill did, a year before Churchill warily included Hitler in his book, *Great Contemporaries*.

Hitler's ambassador in Washington during the mid-thirties, Hans Dieckhoff, an intelligent emissary despite being the brother-in-law of the boorish Foreign Minister von Ribbentrop, continually warned Hitler that Roosevelt had a 'pathological hatred' of Hitler and Mussolini and that Roosevelt was a 'peculiarly dominating personality' who might well seek and win an unprecedented third term in the White House. Roosevelt withdrew his ambassador from Berlin after the *Kristallnacht* anti-Jewish pogrom in 1938. Hitler retaliated in kind, although the First Secretary, Hans Thomsen, continued to warn his government that Roosevelt would win a third term and then use his powers as Commander-in-Chief of the armed forces to provoke an outbreak of hostilities with Germany.

Roosevelt had urged the 'quarantine' of Germany, Italy and Japan in October 1937. On 21 January 1939, he told the Senate Military Affairs Committee that 'France is the actual frontier of America in an apparently inevitable showdown between democracies and dictatorships'. Just before the Nazi–Soviet Pact was signed in August 1939, Roosevelt cabled Stalin that Hitler was certain to attack Russia once he had conquered France. Roosevelt reacted less strenuously to the Russian attack on Finland in December 1939 than Neville Chamberlain and the French Premier Édouard Daladier (and Churchill) did – though he violently disapproved of it – because he knew that the British and French couldn't defeat Hitler without the Russians.

Once Churchill replaced Chamberlain, the Dunkirk operation had succeeded, and the British had shot up the French navy at Oran, Roosevelt finally had the purposeful British leader he had so missed in Ramsay MacDonald, Stanley Baldwin and Chamberlain. Roosevelt had not liked Churchill when they met in 1919, but he admired his anti-Munich stance and had initiated direct contact with him as soon as Churchill returned to the Admiralty in September 1939.

After the fall of France Roosevelt never imagined that Britain could defeat Germany and Italy by herself. When Lord Halifax arrived in the United States as British ambassador in January 1941, he brought with him several senior naval and military officers to begin joint staff talks with the Americans. It was understood then – almost a year before the event – and never altered, that if the US entered the war the primary enemy would be Germany, and not, under any circum-stances, Japan.

Germany, including the conquered territories it directly ruled, had a larger population than the United States, though barely sixty per cent of the population of what was then effectively the Greater Germany actually spoke German. Roosevelt knew that British resistance, heroic though it was, could not continue for ever, especially if other great powers did not join her in the struggle against Germany. He also knew that Hitler's Greater Germany had to be dismantled if Germany were not to become the world's greatest power and fascist dictatorship more fashionable than democracy.

Roosevelt had used the war emergency as a justification for accepting a carefully rigged but supposedly spontaneous draft for renomination as President in 1940, as he set out to break a tradition against a third presidential term that was as old as the republic itself. As the war began and yielded a sequence of German victories, he secured a series of massive defence procurement bills and repeal of the neutrality legis-lation. In the midst of the 1940 election campaign he intro-duced the first peacetime conscription in American history, which he called a 'muster' and which took the form of a lottery. He also sent fifty elderly but serviceable destroyers to the UK in exchange for ninety-nine-year leases on several bases in the Caribbean and Newfoundland.

In 1940 Roosevelt stood for re-election at the head of a broad coalition favouring peace through aid to the democracies and a huge rearmament programme. This coalition extended from the Theodore Roosevelt Republicans through such officially neutral figures as Archbishop Francis Spellman of New York, almost all of Hollywood, and most of America's most distinguished cultural figures, such as John Dewey, John Steinbeck, Albert Einstein, and Sinclair Lewis. With consummate political dexterity, Roosevelt had ditched the liberal isolationists and replaced them as domestic allies with Southern pro-defence internationalists. The colossal rearmament programme and conscription finished off the economic Depression.

The war enabled Roosevelt to promote a defence plan that would turn the United States into the greatest military power in the history of the world. He laid down no fewer than twenty-four aircraft carriers in 1940, and converted nine heavy cruisers under construction into aircraft carriers on the slipways in 1941. (There were then only twenty-five aircraft carriers in the world.) He planned for a navy bigger than Britain's and Japan's combined, an air force twice Britain's and Germany's combined, an army of 300 divisions, and war production sufficient to arm the fighting democracies to the teeth. Roosevelt continued to promise peace through strength and repeatedly said, 'Your President says we are not going to war.' The proverbial 'decent interval' followed the 1940 election, but then came Lend-Lease, by which first the British and then the Russians, Chinese and others were loaned immense quantities of arms and materiel.

It now seems likely that the determining factor in Hitler's decision to attack Russia was his fear of being at war with Britain and the United States while vulnerable to attack from Stalin at the same time. He appears to have reasoned that if he could knock Russia out of the war, he would be able to keep the British and Americans at bay permanently. In the midst of the 1940 election campaign, Roosevelt had accelerated the process of extending US territorial waters out from three miles ultimately to 1,800 miles, which he declared a 'neutrality zone'. Within this zone he ordered the United States to reveal *en clair*, i.e. to the British and Canadian navies, the presence of any German or Italian ship, and from October 1941 to attack any such ship on detection. Thus he made war against one side while giving war-making capabilities on a vast scale to the other. All of this, as was much remarked upon at the time, was a highly idiosyncratic definition of neutrality.

When Roosevelt sent Harry Hopkins to England in January 1941, Hopkins told Winston Churchill that the 'President is determined that we shall win the war together. Make no mistake about it. He has sent me here to tell you that at all costs and by all means, he will carry you through, no matter what happens to him.' It was in this visit to Britain that Hopkins famously said to Churchill, spontaneously, that when he returned to the United States he would tell Roosevelt that in his view, the US should feel towards Britain that: 'Whither thou goest I shall go, where thou lodgest, I shall lodge. Your people shall be my people and your God my God, even to the end.' In his next visit to Britain, in July 1941, Hopkins broadcast from Chequers to say that he had come to Britain on a bomber, in a flight of twenty bombers that were handed over to Britain on landing. He said that those planes 'may tonight be dropping bombs on Brest, on Hamburg, on Berlin, safeguarding our common heritage. Our President is at one with your Prime Minister in his determination to break the ruthless power of that sinful psychopath in Berlin.' These were not neutral comments.

As Hopkins explained to Churchill in February 1941, there were four distinct blocs of American public opinion: ten to fifteen per cent who were Nazi or Communist sympathisers who sheltered behind isolationists like Charles Lindbergh, professed neutrality but wanted a German victory (though polls showed only about five per cent of Americans actually favoured German victory); fifteen to twenty per cent represented by such people as Joseph Kennedy, who wanted to help Britain but were pessimistic and wanted no risk of American entry into the war; ten to fifteen per cent, including Roosevelt's Republican War and Navy Secretaries (Henry Stimson and Frank Knox), and most of the officers, who thought war inevitable and wanted to get on with it; and fifty to sixty per cent who wanted to give all possible aid to Britain even if it risked war, but would prefer not to go to war.

Roosevelt was solidly established at the head of the majority bloc, but also was the preferred candidate of the war party, and retained a share of the Kennedy group. (He managed to dragoon Kennedy into supporting him just before the 1940 election, even though Kennedy had returned to the United States to oppose Roosevelt, who accepted his resignation as ambassador to the Court of St James's only a few days after the election.) Roosevelt thus retained the support of about three-quarters of the American people, a remarkable achievement in such a complicated situation.

Hopkins explained to Churchill that Roosevelt was more or less in the war party himself, but knew the necessity of leading a united country to what would undoubtedly be a far more costly struggle in human terms than was the US's nineteen-month cameo appearance in the First World War. When they finally met, at Argentia, Newfoundland in August 1941, Roosevelt told Churchill he would 'make war on Hitler without declaring it'.

German–American relations continued to deteriorate through the late summer and autumn of 1941. On 4 September 1941, a German submarine fired two torpedoes at the American destroyer *Greer*, near Iceland. Roosevelt spoke to the nation a week later and gave a rather bowdlerised version of the encounter, omitting the fact that the American destroyer had been shadowing the German submarine for the British, who had depth-charged it, and that the *Greer* had then also depth-charged it. (All three navies missed their targets.) It was in this address that Roosevelt announced that America would hear no more 'tender whisperings of appeasers that Hitler is not interested in the Western Hemisphere; no soporific lullabies that a wide ocean separates us from him'. He accused Hitler, rather implausibly, of 'piracy', and announced that henceforth the United States would attack on detection any German or Italian vessel.

On 17 October 1941 the US destroyer *Kearny* – which had gone to the aid of a British convoy – was torpedoed by a German submarine and eleven crewmen were killed. Ten days later Roosevelt gave a Navy Day address broadcast internationally in which he declared: 'The shooting has started. And history has recorded who fired the first shot. In the long run, however, all that will matter is who fired the last shot ... We Americans have cleared our decks and taken out battle stations.' He imputed fantastic ambitions to Hitler in Latin America and the next day added the Soviet Union to the Lend-Lease programme. He had been seeking a pretext to do this ever since Averell Harriman, on Roosevelt's instructions, had promised Stalin massive Lend-Lease assistance several weeks before.

On 30 October, a German submarine torpedoed and sank the American destroyer *Reuben James* off Iceland, killing 115 American sailors, including all the ship's officers. Neutrality was now little more than a fig leaf, with Roosevelt loudly proclaiming to national audiences that the German Chancellor was a 'madman'. More than a month before Pearl Harbor, therefore, Roosevelt was attacking German ships, if they were detected, across most of the North Atlantic, and giving Britain and Russia anything they asked for, including huge quantities of aircraft and tanks, without any real expectation of being paid for them. From all this, and from a mass of further corroborative evidence that could be cited, it is clear that Roosevelt recognised Nazi Germany as a direct threat to the United States and to Western civilisation from early on, and that he thought war likely from 1936, and that after the fall of France the participation of the USSR and the United States would be necessary to win the war against Germany.

By the autumn of 1941, polls showed that seventy per cent of Americans thought it was more important to defeat Germany than to stay out of the war. This was a complete turnaround since the quarantine speech of four years before. The same polls showed a heavy majority for taking a strong line against Japan, not because Americans were particularly preoccupied with China but because they didn't like Japanese bellicosity and moreover they subscribed to the caricature of the bandy-legged, rabbit-toothed, bespectacled 'Jap', who could butcher innocent Chinese but was more adept at making paper fans or plastic flowers than waging war against a serious adversary.

The emergence of Japan as a method of American entry into the war was a late development. Roosevelt had taken a strong stand and thoroughly humbled Japan when the Japanese sank the American gunboat *Panay* in December 1937. He secured reparations and an abject apology. He had followed the policy of Hoover's Secretary of State Henry Stimson, who from 1940 was Roosevelt's War Secretary, of not recognising territorial changes achieved by force. In order to discourage Japan from continuing its aggression in China he embargoed oil and scrap metal (the basics of steel production) to Japan in 1940, other than that which could be obtained by special export permit. Japan imported seventy-five per cent of its oil from the United States and had only an eighteen-month supply. When Roosevelt met Churchill at Argentia in August 1941, Churchill pressed him for an absolute embargo on the sale of oil to Japan and an ultimatum against further aggressive expansion. Churchill had Thailand, the Dutch East Indies and the British positions in Malaya and Hong Kong in mind. Roosevelt declined, saying that it was better to embargo aviation fuel and retain some influence on the Japanese by allowing them some other oil purchases.

Only when he returned to Washington did the President discover that there was an outright oil embargo because the Assistant Secretary of State for Economic Affairs, Dean Acheson, recently returned to government after being sacked by Roosevelt in 1933, had taken it upon himself to refuse any export permits for the sale of oil to Japan. Roosevelt reviewed this policy with his Secretary of State, Cordell Hull, on 5 September. He generally excluded Hull from European affairs, where he thought him too cautious, but Hull was very assertive about Japan. Together they decided to retain the full embargo.

Having told the Japanese ambassador, Admiral Nomura, on 17 August that he would be prepared to meet the Japanese Prime Minister, Prince Konoye, at Honolulu or Juneau, Roosevelt had the State Department tell the Japanese on 2 October that there was no point to such a meeting until Japan accepted Hull's so-called 'Four Principles'. These consisted of requiring Japan to withdraw from China, except for Manchuria, and from Indochina and from the clause of its alliance with Germany and Italy that required Japan to go to war against the United States if war broke out for any reasons between Germany or Italy and the US. The Konoye government fell on 17 October, and was replaced by a belligerent regime headed by General Tojo.

This started the countries' accelerated descent to war as there was no possibility of Japan accepting such humiliating terms. This descent was only interrupted when Roosevelt, on 17 November, had Hull outline to Nomura, a reasonable man, and to Saburo Kurusu, a fanatical militarist who had been sent to reinforce Nomura, a *'modus vivendi'*, as Roosevelt called it. Under this plan, for six months but renewable, some level of exports of rice, oil, and scrap metal would be revived.

The Japanese would send no more military forces to Manchuria or Indochina, would refrain from hostile acts toward British and Dutch territories and Thailand, and negotiations would begin between China and Japan.

The consideration of Roosevelt's offer delayed the Japanese march to war by about two weeks, as the American decryption of the Japanese diplomatic code revealed. But, under protests from Churchill and Chiang Kai-shek, Roosevelt withdrew his *modus vivendi* and negotiations finished with Hall's 'Four Principles' and the equally inflexible Japanese Plan B, that required the United States virtually to legitimise Japanese aggression in China while opening up Dutch East Indian (Indonesian) oil supplies to Japan.

In maintaining the full oil embargo in September and withdrawing his *modus vivendi* in November, Roosevelt was effectively deliberately choosing to enter the war through the Pacific, since the exchange of fire with Hitler in the Atlantic had not produced a full *casus belli*. Roosevelt might have calculated (correctly) that the Germans would honour their obligation to go to war against the United States if Japan did. American cryptologists may have got a hint of this in the November and December diplomatic traffic between Berlin and Tokyo.

This does not add any credibility to the outrageous allegation that Roosevelt and his high command knew an attack was coming specifically at Pearl Harbor and failed to warn the local commanders adequately. General Marshall and Admiral Stark had been sending dire warnings to all commands for many weeks and they were badly let down by the commanders in Hawaii. There was no excuse for not having torpedo nets out around, and some steam up at all times in the battle fleet, and air patrols in all daylight hours 200 miles out from Oahu in all directions. Such elementary measures would have drastically reduced the damage the US Pacific Fleet sustained and Roosevelt had every right to expect that standard of military judgement from his senior officers. Stark had sent the Pacific Fleet commander, Admiral Kimmel, a summary of the damage the British did to the Italian battle fleet at the equally shallow anchorage of Taranto almost exactly a year before with the primitive torpedo aircraft from one aircraft carrier. Kimmel and the Hawaiian air commander, General Short, seem to have ignored the warning. When first advised of the attack at Hawaii, Roosevelt assumed that the air defences at Pearl Harbor were in a state of full readiness.

Roosevelt's original plan had been to await the build-up of colossal military forces in American hands, the further enervation of Germany in Russia and Africa, and to stay out of war in the Pacific, before forcing the issue with Hitler. Had Japan not attacked, this is probably the course he would have followed. It seems that what caused him to change his mind was fear that without an American entry into the war, Russia might have made peace with Germany, signing another treaty along the lines of the 1918 Brest-Litovsk pact or worse, thus entrenching Hitler in most of Europe, leaving him free to attack in Africa or even India and to defend his conquests against the British and Americans. There was also the fear that Chinese resistance, such as it was, would have collapsed if Japan had not been compelled to attack southwards to secure its oil supply. Roosevelt presumably reasoned, on the basis of what Stalin had recently told Hopkins and Harriman, that with America in the war, Russia would fight on even if Moscow fell, as it had against Napoleon. Yet if Russia left the war, it would be practically impossible to recruit it as an ally against Hitler again.

If Japan had accepted Hull's 'Four Principles' and contented itself with continued occupation of Korea, Manchuria and Taiwan, Roosevelt would have focused all his attention on getting directly to grips with Hitler. As it seemed by 'the day of infamy', 7 December 1941, that Russia would hold the Germans before Moscow and Leningrad, he could have made encouraging noises to Stalin and been confident of an undisturbed further build-up at least to the spring of 1942, by which time American warplane production was running at an astounding annual rate of over 100,000 as well as 75,000 tanks, and over 10,000,000 tons of merchant shipping. Without acquiring the Japanese as an active ally, Hitler would presumably have been more reluctant than ever to go to war with the United States, at least while the Soviet Union remained unsubdued. Roosevelt's next steps would presumably have been to send vast quantities of war supplies to Russia in US flagships, much of it right under the noses of the Germans, to Murmansk. He would also have paid and equipped large numbers of volunteers from the British and French empires, and fugitives from the conquered peoples of Europe, and a huge anti-fascist international brigade, doubtless including a good many Americans, to fight in Russia and Egypt. He would also have supplied Britain with enough aircraft and assisted in the training of enough pilots to conduct as comprehensive a bombing campaign against Germany as the Anglo-Americans did in 1943 and 1944.

If that didn't push Hitler over the brink into war, Roosevelt would have had to move before Hitler and Stalin recomposed their differences, as they had in 1939. In pursuit of the destruction of Nazism, Roosevelt, the political shaman, could have been counted upon to be fiendishly imaginative, and he would have needed to move well before the 1944 election. Without a direct attack from Hitler, Roosevelt would have had to act with less than the absolutely united opinion that he learned from Woodrow Wilson was necessary in going to war and which Pearl Harbor gave him.

It would have been more like the somewhat unstable public opinion Madison and Lincoln had to contend with, but by the spring of 1943 the United States would have had an immense navy and air force – as it did in fact – and the army would have grown to over 200 divisions. Without the Japanese to contend with, roughly the same timetable that was followed in the European war would have been achievable, even with a later starting date. Most of the 100 Army and Marine divisions that were in the Pacific in 1944 could have been deployed in Europe.

Even if Hitler had continued to observe a Job-like patience, which is unlikely given the eagerness with which he declared war on the United States after Pearl Harbor, a leader of Roosevelt's ingenuity and determination would have done whatever was necessary to bring his country into the war and dispose of the Nazis. Having, with the help of Churchill's eloquence and Hitler's barbarism, brought his countrymen from profound isolationism to the verge of interventionism in four years, he would certainly have completed the trajectory in another two.

A collision between Hitler and Roosevelt was practically inevitable from their almost simultaneous assumption of the headship of their countries. Japan was a means to an end. Without it, Roosevelt would have found another means to the same end. He knew Nazi Germany and the Western democracies could not coexist. He was right.

The Brighton Bomb Kills Margaret Thatcher

Simon Heffer

As dawn broke over Brighton on the morning of Friday 12 October 1984 the full extent of the carnage wrought by the massive IRA bomb in the Grand Hotel became immediately apparent. Rescue teams swarmed over piles of smoking rubble. Although many of those in the building when the bomb exploded had escaped with varying degrees of injury, the emergency services were unsure how many who had not been killed in the initial blast had failed to get out of the building before almost all of it collapsed fifteen minutes after the explosion.

In its menacing admission of having planted the Brighton bomb, the Irish Republican Army warned the British Prime Minister, Margaret Thatcher: 'Today we were unlucky, but remember we only have to be lucky once.' The explosion had left six people attending the Tory Party Conference dead, among them the wife of the Chief Whip, John Wakeham. Wakeham himself was seriously injured, as was his colleague Norman Tebbit, the Trade and Industry Secretary. Tebbit's wife, Margaret, was never able to walk again. The real target of the bombers, Mrs Thatcher, was shocked but physically unscathed. She addressed her supporters as planned the following afternoon. Had the explosion been a little more powerful, and taken her life and those of some of her senior colleagues staying in the rooms around her, the subsequent history of the Tory Party, Great Britain and quite possibly the world would have been very different.

Mrs Thatcher had led the Conservatives to a landslide victory over Michael Foot's Labour Party in June 1983. Her first term had seen, principally, the passage of legislation abolishing the legal immunities of trade unions, and victory over Argentina in the Falklands War. The big theme of her second term was privatisation of the nationalised industries, reducing the size of the state and continuing the process of cutting taxes. The National Union of Mineworkers had declared a strike without a ballot the previous spring, and this was still in progress.

There was a continuing problem with Northern Ireland, and the recently retired Secretary of State for the Province, Jim Prior, had been urging more constructive engagement with the Irish Republic over lessening tensions in Ulster. Prior had left the government shortly before the Brighton conference to become chairman of the electrical giant GEC; his successor, Douglas Hurd, was ideologically sympathetic to Prior's approach, but by the time of the bombing had had little chance to take any initiatives in his new post.

Shortly before the conference an opinion poll among Conservative supporters asked whom they would most have liked to succeed Mrs Thatcher were a vacancy to occur. The most popular candidate was Norman Tebbit, with Michael Heseltine in second place. Had the Brighton bombing achieved its aim that decision would have had to be made far earlier than anyone expected; but it would not, at that stage, have been taken with any reference to the party's rank and file. The choice would have been made by the party's 390 or so Members of Parliament.

Unless the bomb had wrought wider damage and killed Tebbit too, he would have been available. He would, though, have still been hospitalised at the time of a leadership contest, and it would have been far from certain that he would ever again enjoy sufficient health to hold the office of Prime Minister. Moreover, the severity of his wife's injuries would clearly have placed enormous strains on any attempt by Tebbit to play a prominent role in public life. This turned out to be the case in fact, when to great surprise, and having chaired the party at the time of the 1987 election victory, he announced his retirement from the government just as many were expecting him to be offered, and to accept, a great office of state.

What is certain is that however violent the bombing might have been, it would not have harmed Heseltine. At the moment of the explosion he was in Rome attending a NATO summit, as Secretary of State for Defence. The only obstacle, therefore, to his succeeding to the leadership and the premiership would have been the good favour of his colleagues. The Cabinet's elder statesman, Viscount Whitelaw, would also not have been harmed by the bomb, since he was staying with a friend some miles from Brighton. Although he was the Deputy Prime Minister, a constitutional precedent then dating back over eighty years would have prevented him, as a peer, from being Prime Minister.

With Tebbit badly injured, it is far from clear who the 'Thatcherite' candidate would have been in the fight against Heseltine. Cecil Parkinson had, just a year earlier, been the darling of the party; but his resignation at the time of the 1983 conference, after he admitted fathering a child by his secretary, would have appeared to put him out of the running. Nigel Lawson, the Chancellor of the Exchequer, lacked the popularity among MPs to be a realistic leadership candidate. So, too, did the Home Secretary, Leon Brittan.

Sir Keith Joseph, the Education Secretary, was the closest ideologically to Mrs Thatcher of any of her Cabinet colleagues. However, the perceived other-worldliness that had prevented him from challenging Edward Heath for the leadership in 1975 would have made him an unlikely contender in 1984, not least against so ruthless and technocratic an opponent as Heseltine. Sir Geoffrey Howe, the Foreign Secretary, was not at that time held so high in the affections of the parliamentary party as he later became, and in any case the temperamental resistance to taking the leadership that caused him to back Heseltine against Mrs Thatcher in 1990 would doubtless have manifested itself six years earlier. Also, in considering the claims of other possible candidates, one must bear in mind that if the blast had been better targeted or more powerful so that it killed Mrs Thatcher, it would probably have killed her most senior colleagues, whose rooms were in the same area of the first floor of the Grand Hotel; so the field might have been extremely limited.

Failing an organised 'stop Heseltine' movement, such as occurred in 1990, the Defence Secretary would therefore probably have won a leadership contest held in November 1984. An attempt to stop him at any price would have been unlikely. Although regarded as a corporatist and inter- ventionist, he had taken pains to pursue elements of the Thatcher agenda sufficiently to keep him in sympathy – superficially – with the mainstream of the party. Most import- ant, he would not have been stigmatised by many Tories with the label of 'assassin', as he was in 1990. The vacancy for which he would have competed in 1984 would have been created by a literal and not a metaphorical assassination, and one in which he had had no hand.

Heseltine's combined gifts of self publicity and self- projection would have helped him to find the right language to soothe and hold together a party that had lost not just its revered leader, but also quite possibly several other senior ministers. However tasteless or ironic such an observation might be, there could probably have been no more propitious circumstances in which Heseltine might have achieved his ambition of becoming Leader of the Conservative Party and Prime Minister. After such a tragedy, the goodwill behind him would have been immense, and he would have enjoyed a honeymoon period far longer than his talents or his position in the party's ideological coalition would normally have allowed him.

However, almost from the start one theme would have run through this administration, and that would have been the progressive alienation of the most ardent Thatcherites in the Conservative movement. This process would have begun with Heseltine's likely appointments to his Cabinet, and the structural reforms of government in which he had always expressed an interest. Those two processes would, of course, have been closely linked. In his 1987 book *Where There's a Will*, Heseltine outlined his personal manifesto for the governance of Britain.

Despite the disaster it had been in practice, the experiment by the Wilson government of having a Department of Economic Affairs to rival the Treasury was one Heseltine felt had potential. The Wilson experiment, with George Brown as the Secretary of State for Economic Affairs, failed in Heseltine's view because of personal conflicts within the Labour Cabinet. Heseltine seemed to imagine that no such conflict would have occurred in his administration, or at least that he would have had the force of personality as Prime Minister to prevent it. So whomever Heseltine appointed as Chancellor would have had to cope with a Department of Economic Affairs dealing directly with business and discharging a general, and nebulous, brief to ensure that the economic conditions would have been as favourable as possible for the private sector. Whatever Heseltine's expectations, this would soon have caused as much trouble under a Tory government as under a Labour one.

Heseltine is on record repeatedly as an opponent of planning; but planning was the *raison d'être* of the old DEA, with Brown sending out questionnaires to businessmen asking them to predict what they would be selling three or five years hence. Heseltine paid lip service to the free market in many of his pronouncements, but failed to grasp that activities of the sort a DEA could have been expected to undertake would have been better suited to a command economy rather than a free one. Wilson abandoned the idea of a DEA within a couple of years, not least because it proved unworkable and unnecessary. Only Heseltine's own conceitedness would prevent him from doing the same.

Heseltine had, of course, been a successful businessman in

his own right, but some of his own methods (as exposed by his biographers) were hardly those he could recommend to everyone else: such as remaining solvent by not paying your bills until your creditors are on the verge of legal action against you to recover the debt. Despite his commercial experience, he found it hard to predict accurately the nature of the development of the British economy. He did not foresee the service boom, and his determination to keep manufacturing on a life-support machine ignored the realities of the huge fixed costs in the European economy, and their inability to compete with the low-wage economies of China, Indonesia and elsewhere in the developing Far East.

Heseltine's other structural aim would have been to increase the status, and develop the role, of the Department of Trade and Industry. His aggrandised view of this department was seen in practice when he returned to office under John Major and, in 1992, took over the DTI, promptly assuming the obsolete title of President of the Board of Trade. He wrote in *Where There's a Will*: 'I hope in this book to dispel the false belief which has misled too many in my party, that there is a heresy called "intervention" to which unsound Conservatives have in the past been prone but which sound Conservative administrations eschew.' He dismissed this as 'too romantic and impractical [*sic*] a guide for men and women who hold public office, and it has nothing to do with the Tory party'. This was a view with which the bulk of the party, and the orthodoxy that he would have inherited, would violently have disagreed.

Showing, again, a resolute determination not to learn from the mistakes of previous prime ministers, Heseltine saw little to disagree with in the failed industrial policy of the Heath government. His view of the success stories of the world economy in 1986–7, when he was writing *Where There's a Will*, was based on equally false assumptions. He wanted to emulate Japan and Germany, economies that within a few years of his writing were in crisis caused by over-regulation, reliance on cartels and protectionism, and institutionalised uncompetitiveness. Despite the trouble Heath had had with his intervention to prop up Rolls-Royce, Heseltine saw no problem with subsidising, for example, the car industry, even though it could not sell its goods, was producing cars of inferior quality, and despite the self-evident fact that public money could be better used elsewhere – such as by being left in the pockets of private individuals to make their own investment decisions. Even though the National Economic Development Organisation (eventually abolished by Mrs Thatcher) showed no evidence of doing anything to develop the economy at all, Heseltine wanted this talking-shop for ministers, industrialists and trade unionists to be given even greater weight.

The tripartite squabbles between a Treasury that would have to pay for such indulgences, a DEA that would be arguing for the rigging of markets to improve the performance of subsidised industries, and a Board of Trade that would be combing the country searching for new lame ducks to pump scarce resources into might have jolted the Prime Minister back towards reality. However, someone who still saw the Heath government as an administration dogged by bad luck rather than by economic ignorance and poor decision-making would not have been quickly convinced of the viability of the more laissez-faire alternatives. Also, the personnel that Heseltine would have been likely to choose as his closest colleagues would not have been among the first to dissent from his Heathite philosophy.

Of the practising politicians of the time, none was more revered by Heseltine than Peter Walker, from whom he had learned much of his own ideology in the late 1960s and early 1970s. Although a successful businessman, Walker was a devotee of the neo-socialist, postwar consensus views that so held back British industry between 1945 and 1979 under governments of both colours. Like Heseltine and, indeed, Heath, Walker was a pseudo-intellectual whose economic views were informed mostly by sentiment rather than by logic or empiricism. He would probably have been offered whichever post Heseltine felt most essential to the success of his administration – either the Chancellorship or the Board of Trade.

Heseltine might have been expected to try to tempt Jim Prior – another politician in the same mould – back from GEC, and might even have succeeded were the job on offer to have been senior enough. There might also have been a recall in some capacity for Sir Ian Gilmour, who would at least have helped give genuine intellectual ballast to the administration. Meanwhile, others associated with the Thatcherite programme might have been sidelined, or resigned. It would have been hard to imagine, for example, Nigel Lawson accepting the diminished role of the Treasury and staying as Chancellor, and the social liberals around Heseltine might have found Leon Brittan altogether too astringent to stay at the Home Office.

The Thatcherite legacy would not have been entirely abandoned. Heseltine claimed to support privatisation, the selling of council houses to their tenants and the extension of the principle of wider share ownership. It is reasonable to believe that he would have pursued the further selling-off of nationalised industries. He subscribed, under collective responsibility, to the Thatcher government's methods in dealing with the miners' strike, so it is reasonable to suppose that he would have taken a similar course – not least with the memory of Heath's defeat by the miners a decade earlier still relatively fresh. He also had one 'big idea' that applied the tenets of Thatcherism to the civil service.

Heseltine argued, in *Where There's a Will*, for a reform of Whitehall which would have given each permanent secretary personnel functions, ending centralised pay-scales and jobs for life. Market rates would have been available to pay the salaries of specialists, under the scrutiny of the National Audit Office. This would have helped achieve Heseltine's other, laudable, aim of encouraging people with a track record of success in the private sector into the civil service later in their careers. It would also have set an example for the reform of local government that would have helped cut bureaucracy and rigidities. However, the Heseltine administration's determination to limit the effect of the free market, to 'pick winners' rather than allow enterprise to find its own way, and above all to soak the productive sectors of the economy in order to keep afloat the unproductive ones would have, in all probability, led to a slowing-down of the economy in the mid- to late-1980s compared with what happened under Thatcherism.

The biggest difference compared with the Thatcher programme – and the policy that would have had the most profound consequences for a Heseltine administration – would have been in relation to Europe. Heseltine was a committed European in the mould of Heath. There would have been no hesitation about forcing through the Single European Act in 1986, just indeed as there was none by the Thatcher government. Where the big difference would have emerged would have been in the British attitude to the European Exchange Rate Mechanism. Probably without much debate or any wider consultation – as it would be an extremely market-sensitive act – Heseltine would have been inclined to join this system of fixed exchange rates shortly after a likely election victory in 1987 or 1988. This would have opened up a wide internal split in his party two or three years before it actually came. As with the actual process of shadowing the Deutschmark, and then joining the ERM, this would have led to a level of interest rates being imposed on Britain that was unsuited to the domestic conditions of the British economy, with a resultant contraction in growth.

Another consequence of Mrs Thatcher's death might have been a slower progress towards the dismantling of the Soviet empire, and the delayed reunification of Germany, which imposed such strains on Britain during her actual membership of the ERM in the early 1990s. Although Heseltine was pro-American insofar as he understood the importance of America as the guarantor of Western European security during the Cold War, he showed no predilection for Ronald Reagan, nor so great a commitment to the 'special relationship' as Mrs Thatcher had. It was the combination of Anglo-American pressure on Mikhail Gorbachev, as well as the empathy between the Soviet leader and Mrs Thatcher, that helped create the unstoppable momentum that lifted the Iron Curtain. With Heseltine in charge in Britain, and with his view of Britain as locked into a European Community designed as a fortress against the Soviet bloc, it is questionable whether that momentum would have come quite so early as it did. Also, he showed no evidence at any time in his career of an understanding of politics in the Soviet bloc; and unlike Mrs Thatcher, he was never driven ideologically by the belief that the irrepressible human instinct for freedom would bring about the end of Soviet communism.

Heseltine's European policy would, however, have proved the ultimate cause of his downfall. The involvement of Britain in the ERM would have created a powerful faction against him. It would also have led to the period of stiflingly high interest rates that occurred at the end of the 1980s coming perhaps two years earlier, and advancing commensurately the loss of the Conservative Party's reputation for economic competence. Yet it would have been the symbolic rather than the practical effects of this policy that would have made enemies for Heseltine. The policy of ERM membership signalled a surrender of sovereignty of a sort to which the Tory Party was never able, and still has not been able, to reconcile itself.

Perhaps Heseltine would have been shrewd, and sought to bind what came to be known as 'Eurosceptics' into his Cabinet and therefore into accepting a share of responsibility for the consequences of his decision. Had he done this, the faction might well have been leaderless, and would have comprised of backbenchers supported by the grass roots. However, Heseltine showed in his political career few examples of making accommodations with those whose views he despised unless it was in the furtherance of his own ambition. Having achieved the ultimate political post, it is hard to imagine he would have imitated Mrs Thatcher's inclusion of the 'wets' in her Cabinet by including many of his ideological enemies in his.

The quarrels that emerged within, crippled and finally smashed the Tory Party in the five years after the Maastricht Treaty was concluded would have been fuelled that much earlier. By 1990 the party would have been an exhibition of disunity and factionalism, the old differences between, effectively, Powellites and Heathites having been exposed by Heseltine's policy. In this context, Heseltine might – like John Major, in fact – have been inclined to wait until 1992 to go to the country rather than conclude a four-year term in 1991.

Such successes as Heseltine's seven years in Downing Street might have brought, in reform of Whitehall and episodic urban regeneration, would by then have been outweighed by higher interest rates, rising unemployment and higher taxes. His schemes of intervention in industry would have proved as fruitless as they were in fact when he ran the Board of Trade between 1992 and 1995. Subsidy of industries to keep them afloat for strategic – or sentimental – reasons would have cost the country much otherwise productive investment, jobs and higher taxation. With no international triumphs to buoy him up, except the unsatisfactory conclusion of the first Gulf War, all this would provide a difficult background against which to seek a second mandate as Prime Minister.

Neil Kinnock only narrowly lost the 1992 election to John Major. Had the Conservative Party already imploded in terms of discipline, as it might well have done by then because of the more precipitate nature of a Heseltine European policy, Kinnock could quite feasibly have won it. Britain's earlier entry into the ERM might also have forced its earlier exit; and if 'Black Wednesday' had happened before an election rather than shortly after it, the Conservatives would have stood no chance at all.

Heseltine's writings and speeches all have an ostensible theme of achieving consensus. In fact, he was throughout his career a highly divisive figure, not least because of the monumental nature of his ego. Pro-Europeanism of the sort he embraced would, given the mood of the Tory Party of the late 1980s, have been little short of suicidal for him, and would have given his internal enemies all the excuse they required to obstruct and, if necessary, attack him.

Always a brilliant rhetorician, Heseltine was less adept at actual achievement. Right from his time as a junior aviation minister in the Heath government – when he and his wife toured the world at public expense to promote Concorde, yet failed to sell a single one – his pre-publicity exceeded the actual results. Particularly if the years after 1987 had been bedevilled by internecine conflicts, the chances of his starting and carrying through wider reforms of institutions and services would have been limited. It would, as in so many of the jobs he actually did, have been a question of holding the line and seeking to maintain momentum by the illusion of initiatives.

So the Tories lose the 1991 or 1992 election, and it is up to Prime Minister Kinnock to ratify the Maastricht Treaty initialled by his Conservative predecessor. It might not have been a heavy defeat, and certainly nothing on the scale of the actual massacre of 1997, but the sizeable faction disobliged by Heseltine's European policy would have laid the blame for the result squarely on him, and on the pursuit of that policy. The Conservatives, in Opposition, would want the freedom to attack the surrenders of sovereignty that would be forced upon Mr Kinnock. This might have proved a popular line with the public, not least when it became clear to them that the economic stringencies suffered as a result of the

Heseltine policy would become even worse under a high-spending, unreformed Labour government that was black-mailed back into a fixed-exchange-rate system, with its resulting inflexibilities.

A defeat in 1992 for the Tories could well have seen them back in power by 1996 or 1997. The two landslide defeats of 1997 and 2001 would probably never have happened. John Major would probably never have happened either, with the party looking at someone like Michael Portillo – then still ostensibly a right-wing Eurosceptic – to lead them after Heseltine's departure.

Yet the ultimate price paid for Mrs Thatcher's death in 1984 would have been the failure to complete her programme, and therefore the failure to impress upon the Labour Party that it needed to respect the new consensus she had forged. Britain would have been set as a highly taxed, inefficient country like modern France, Germany or Japan, inadequately using its human and capital resources. That, and the increasing failure of Britain to make its way in a world ruled by economic methods and political forces that a deep-seated Keynesian and European like Heseltine simply could not come to grips with, would have been his disastrous legacy.

The Chads Fall Off in Florida

David Frum

> Presidential Emergency Operations Center,
> Underneath the White House
> 11 September 2001, 11.43 a.m.

The voice of President Al Gore is heard through a speakerphone, over the noise of the engines of Air Force One.

President Gore: 'So what do we know?'

National Security Adviser Leon Fuerth: 'It's got al Qaeda's fingerprints all over it. Positive identification will have to wait for more information, but for now, we must assume that this is a bin Laden job.'

Gore: 'Like the Cole – and the embassy bombings in '98.'

Fuerth: 'Yes sir.'

Gore: 'I suppose this time we'll actually have to do something?'

Fuerth: 'I'm afraid so, sir.'

Gore: 'Kind of makes you feel bad that we dusted off Sudan's offer to finger him to the CIA.'

Fuerth: 'No sir, that was the right call. The Sudanese wanted us to come in guns blasting and scoop him up the way the French scooped up Carlos the Jackal. But what about bin Laden's wives and children? They could have been hurt. And besides, our evidence against him would not have stood up in a court of law. Intelligence materials are not admissible in criminal cases, and if we'd tried to change that rule, all the civil liberties organisations would have squawked. You pride yourself on your civil liberties record, Mr President. So what would you have done with the Sudanese information? Assassinate him? We discussed that again and again in the 1990s,

179

Mr President, and we agreed that while it was OK if bin Laden got killed in the course of military action, it was not OK to deliberately target him. We can't allow ourselves to stoop to French tactics, Mr President.'

Gore: 'No, I suppose not. So what are our options now?'

Secretary of State Richard Holbrooke: 'We've drafted a very tough resolution which we can send to the Security Council immediately. It condemns terrorism in unequivocal terms, and urges the government of Afghanistan immediately to surrender bin Laden and the leadership of al Qaeda to the jurisdiction of the International Criminal Court.'

Gore: 'Good thing we ratified that treaty this spring – otherwise I don't know who'd have jurisdiction to try bin Laden. What's the maximum sentence the ICC can impose?'

Holbrooke: 'Twenty-five years – subject to time off for good behaviour of course. But I have to warn you sir, there may be some evidentiary problems.'

Gore: 'What kind of problems?'

Holbrooke: 'Well the Taliban say that they will only surrender bin Laden if we can assure them that his trial will be in accordance with the principles of Islamic law. That means non-Muslims will not be able to testify. Fortunately, Solicitor General Laurence Tribe has a keen interest in non-Western spirituality, and he has indicated he would be willing to convert to Islam in order to advance the case.'

Gore: 'Good man. But what if we can't win a conviction in the ICC? I mean, some of those Swedish judges – they can be kind of permissive.'

Secretary of Defense Wesley Clark: 'Yes sir. The Joint Chiefs are working on military options right now. I've asked them to work out a plan to capture bin Laden and his henchmen using non-lethal munitions. We're assembling a broad multilateral coalition to go into Afghanistan if need be. UN Secretary General Kofi Annan has proposed some excellent candidates to command the expedition: he highly recommends Gen. Obasawo Okobogo of Senegal – Okobogo is a devout Muslim, so we can count on him to respect local cultural sensitivities.'

Gore: 'How big a force would we need?'

Clark: 'Well sir, we don't want to take any chances. I think we can learn from our mistakes in Kosovo . . .'

Holbrooke: 'Your mistakes . . .'

Clark: '. . . and send ample ground forces. The Joint Chiefs have prepared a plan to send five divisions into Afghanistan, backed by combat aircraft, tanks, self-propelled howitzers and lots and lots of supplies. The earliest it could arrive would be about February 2002. That's the middle of the dreaded Afghan winter, so I recommend we wait until early April, just to be on the safe side.'

Environmental Protection Agency head Carol Browner: 'Mr President, if I may –'

Gore: 'Yes, Carol.'

Browner: 'Sir, you issued an executive order the day after your Inaugural requiring that all proposed military operations undergo environmental review. If we put a force of five divisions into the field in Afghanistan, not to mention all that heavy equipment, we are going to way, way exceed our CO_2 limits for the year.'

Gore: 'That's a serious problem.'

Secretary of the Treasury George Soros: 'Not necessarily, Mr President – we just have to cut back on CO_2 emissions here at home. Before this attack, we were talking about a seventy-five-cent a gallon hike in the gasoline tax. Make it a dollar instead. That will force a drastic reduction in emissions – and we can always use the cash.'

Gore: 'Excellent George, thank you. Listen up everybody: whatever we do, I want this to be the first environmentally sensitive war in history. Wes, you make sure our troops know: they're to watch out for migratory birds when they march. And no littering!'

Clark: 'Yes sir.'

Gore: 'What about the home front? What are we doing to

find if there are any other al Qaeda cells on our soil?'

Attorney General Vernon Jordan: 'Everything we can, sir, within the limits of your executive order banning the use of ethnic, religious, racial, or national origins profiling. We've got 15,000 FBI agents at work; they're starting with everybody in the country whose last name begins with "A" and working downward through the alphabet.'

Gore: 'That's good. But I worry that there are a lot of Arabic names that begin with A – you know, Abu this and that. Could have an unintended differential impact. Why don't we start with the Zs and work our way up?'

Jordan: 'Yes, sir.'

Gore: 'Now, these are bold actions. We're going to need to keep Congress informed and involved. Donna – are you lining up the congressional leaders?'

Donna Brazile, Chief of Staff: 'Yes, sir. Leaders of both parties have offered their full support. They're ready to do whatever you ask.'

Gore: 'Great. Tell them we'll be sending up our plan for universal health insurance next week.'

Brazile: 'Sir? Um, I'm not sure that's exactly the kind of request Congress is expecting. They were thinking more along the lines of, you know, increases to the defence budget . . .'

Gore: 'Arms are for hugging. We can't let this historic moment lapse into just another bonanza for the military-industrial complex. Besides, thousands of people have probably been injured or wounded today. Many thousands more have suffered psychological trauma. I can't think of a better way to respond to these terrorists than by assuring all those wounded – and all those traumatised – that their government is ready to take care of them, and everyone else who is ill, frightened or unhappy.'

Brazile: 'Sir, I agree – but the votes just won't be there in Congress.'

Gore: 'The votes will be there after I address the nation

tonight. You know the effect I have on the American people. When I speak, they will rally. I'll be back in Washington by nightfall. Book time on the networks; I'll need about an hour. I'll talk about national security and health security and environmental security – how they're really all one issue. Get my writers on the job.'

Brazile: 'There's another problem.'

Gore: 'Jeez, Donna, I pay you to solve problems.'

Brazile: 'Sir, if you can find somebody who can solve this problem, you fire me and hire her. It's Clinton.'

Gore: 'That bitch. What's she done now?'

Brazile: 'Not her – her husband. He's up in New York City – and he's been on TV all day. Explaining how hard he worked to prevent this kind of terrorist attack, how focused he was on terrorism through his Administration, how he tried to advise you, how you're doing your best, how much confidence he has that you'll rise to this crisis . . .'

Gore: 'Fuck him too. So what's the problem?'

Brazile: 'Well the networks kind of feel . . . that after so many hours of Clinton, maybe people will feel they have heard enough from . . .'

Gore: 'He's not the President – I am the President.'

Brazile: 'Absolutely, sir, no question about that sir, everyone knows that sir. He says he is just trying to be helpful, to fill in until you decide it is safe for you to return to the capital, because your top priority has to be your personal safety.'

Gore (incredulous, furious): 'He said that to you?'

Brazile (anxious): Yes sir. And to NBC, ABC, CBS, CNN, MSNBC, BBC, al-Jazeera, German TV, French TV – not Fox though. He says he won't talk to just anybody.'

Gore: 'Vernon?'

Jordan: 'Yes, Mr President?'

Gore: 'Have we got anything on the books that would allow us to lock up former president Clinton for a week or two? Maybe a month?'

Jordan: 'I'll look into it.'

Fuerth: 'Sir, if I may: there are some other issues to think about as well. We can't rule out that Saddam Hussein may use the six or seven months till our expeditionary force lands in Afghanistan to make mischief. Would you like me to prepare some options?'

Gore: 'No. Leave Iraq out of it. You know how Chirac feels about Iraq. Just the last time I talked with him he said Iraq was indispensable to economic security.'

Clark: 'France's economic security?'

Gore: 'No, *his* economic security – and this is no moment to start alienating good friends like Jacques Chirac. We've got to bring them along gradually. Let's leave Iraq for Hillary in '09. She's welcome to it.'

Laughter.

Gore: 'OK. What else?'

Brazile: 'We're placing calls to Mayor Giuliani and Governor Pataki – they'll talk as soon as they are able. Alan Greenspan tells us that he's pumping plenty of liquidity into the financial system now – he's confident that the markets and the dollar can weather this blow, but he's keeping a careful eye on Japan and Europe.'

Gore: 'We're going to do everything we can for New York City. This is no time to count pennies. Just make sure that Senator Schumers gets credit for everything. We don't want a certain junior senator grabbing the spotlight. Then I want to talk to the allies: Blair, Chirac, Schroeder, Putin, line them all up for me. Anything else?'

Brazile: 'Tipper's waiting to talk to you – she wants you to know she's safe.'

Gore: 'Thank God. Kiss her for me.'

Brazile: 'Sir, I think that's your department.'

Fuerth: 'Sir, have you thought about what you will say to the allies?'

Gore: 'Yes. I'm going to assure them that we're going to act boldly – but that we're not going to take any crazy risks. They all know me. They know what to expect from me. No surprises. No adventures. Steady as she goes.'

Fuerth: 'They'll like that. I'll get it set up. Next: what about Iran? They've left fingerprints on almost every major anti-American terrorist attack since the early 1980s. We can't make any assumptions about their role here. A lot of our people think that the reason the Iranians are working so hard to develop nuclear missiles is to buy themselves impunity if they're caught in terrorist acts like this one.'

Gore: 'I'm not saying Iran is not a problem. We just have to wait for the threat to become imminent – the way we waited for the threat from bin Laden to become imminent before we took action against him.'

Clark: 'Strictly speaking, sir, the threat from bin Laden is a little bit more than imminent now.'

Gore: 'Fair point. You can't time these things precisely. But I think we can all agree – and I know our European allies will agree – that when it comes to Iraq and Iran, and all the rest, it's better to be a little too late than a little too early. I'll explain that in my speech too. I want to stress the complexities of the situation. I want to tell the nations of the world that they can be with us, or they can be with the terrorists, or they can be somewhere in between. I want to say that we regard these acts as wrong, but we understand that others may take a different view. By the way, can anybody think of a less harsh word than "wrong"? You know how moralistic language upsets the Europeans.'

Vice President Joe Lieberman: 'Mr President, I don't think we should be shy about using the word "wrong". There is a moral dimension to this problem.'

Gore: 'Absolutely. You're right. And I'm not shy. But Joe, remember, we have to make our case convincing to the whole world. To people with many different value systems. While of course expressing our own severe condemnation. Perhaps we could say that we regard these attacks as … "inappropriate".'

Lieberman: 'Inappropriate?'

Gore: (musingly): 'Yeah. We'll want to get the speech-writers on it, but we could say something like, "We urge all the nations of the world to join us in expressing their firm disapproval of these inappropriate acts. These inappropriate acts didn't just harm America; they threaten the peace and security of the whole world." This isn't just America's fight; it's everybody's fight. We want everybody in – and we're prepared to do what everybody says.'

Holbrooke: 'Very eloquent sir!'

Gore: 'Thanks. But as we think about how we're going to present our case to the world, there's a sensitive issue we have to deal with. We're going to need the goodwill and support of the Islamic world. It's vitally important that we respect Muslim sensitivities. And Joe . . .'

Lieberman: 'Yes, Mr President?'

Gore: 'There are a lot of Muslims who think my admin-istration is, well, too Jewish. There's you, there's Leon, there's George, there's Wes . . .'

Clark: 'Only half, Mr President!'

Gore: 'Try telling that to the Saudis, Wes. And of course there's Holbrooke . . .'

Holbrooke (outraged): 'Mr President!'

Gore: 'Don't worry, Richard, your secret is safe with me. But Joe: I'm going to have to ask you to lie low for a little while. We're going to send you to an undisclosed location – not for long, just a few weeks, maybe a couple of months. Just until I've regained the trust of our Muslim friends.'

Lieberman: 'Mr President, shouldn't we worry a little more about their need to regain our trust?'

Gore: 'I understand how you feel, Joe. But this is no time for jingoism. It's a time for healing. Our top priority right now is to understand why these people are so angry at us – and maybe find some way to assuage that anger. We're going to go to work right away on a plan to create a Palestinian state – maybe also to return East Timor to Indonesia and Spain back to Syria. We may have forgotten that Spain used to be ruled from Damascus – but they haven't. And they're still humiliated by the loss.'

Browner: 'Mr President, may I interject here? If I hear you correctly, you're saying there's a crucial psychological dimension to this attack.'

Gore: 'That's right.'

Browner: 'It's kind of like the point you make in your book *Earth in the Balance* about the trauma of the gifted child –'

Holbrooke (rapidly, over-eagerly): 'On page 228.'

Browner: 'You begin life with all this potential and all these expectations –'

Gore: 'Yes, yes, that's exactly right.'

Browner: 'that you inwardly feel you can never live up to –'

Gore: 'This is good.'

Browner: 'and yet you are terrified of letting down your parents –'

Gore: 'Yes! Yes!'

Browner: 'And so you suffer all these doubts, feelings of unworthiness. You act out in unacceptable ways – to try to defy those expectations – but that only intensifies your feelings of unworthiness. Maybe the whole Muslim world is feeling like they have somehow not lived up to their potential and they have to lash out at us. And maybe the most important thing we can do right now is show them that our love and support are unconditional – that they don't have to behave in these unacceptable ways to get our attention – and then help them work through these feelings.'

Gore: 'Carol, if I hear you right, you're saying that this all really comes down to communications issues?'

Browner: 'Yes sir.'

Gore: 'That's really really interesting. People, isn't that interesting?'

All: 'Yes sir! Very interesting sir!'

Gore: 'So where do we take this?'

Browner: 'Well sir, I remember during the campaign that

you once said that you thought that just as we had a National Security Council and a National Economic Council, perhaps we also needed a National Psychological Council that could bring together experts in emotional and gender issues. Maybe this is the right time to get it going. This is a moment when we're going to have to help the American people get past their – justified – feelings of anger and vengefulness. We're going to have to help Islamic people get past their feelings – and we're going to need the best brains out there to tell us how to do it.'

Gore: 'Carol, I love this. I think this is exactly the message the country needs to hear now. Not lashing out – reaching out. Not blaming – understanding. You know I'm not a religious man. But after I won the recount, I thought – this election was so close – it could have gone either way – I didn't get here on my own. God wanted me in this job. But why? I kept turning and turning the question over in my mind. And now I know: I'm here to give our generation a second chance to stand up for our principles – to wage peace, to show understanding, to be the kind of America the world wants us to be.

All right, I think that wraps things up. Anything else you need to tell me before I talk to Tipper?'

Brazile: 'Oh yes – Governor Bush called. He wants you to know that he's praying for you.'

Gore: 'I bet he is. Jesus. Bush. I wonder if he can even find Afghanistan on the map. Can't you just imagine the mess he'd make if he were sitting in this chair right now?'

Brazile: 'Yeah. Thank God for Florida.'

All: 'Amen.'